CW00543400

EVERYDAY
LEBANESE
COOKING

EVERYDAY
LEBANESE
COOKING

Mona Hamadeh

A HOW TO BOOK

ROBINSON

For my Mum

ROBINSON

First published in Great Britain in 2013 by Spring Hill,
an imprint of Constable & Robinson Ltd
This edition published in 2013 by Robinson

5 7 9 10 8 6

Copyright © Mona Hamadeh 2013

The moral right of the author has been asserted.

All rights reserved.
No part of this publication may be reproduced, stored in a retrieval system, or transmitted, in any form, or by any means, without the prior permission in writing of the publisher, nor be otherwise circulated in any form of binding or cover other than that in which it is published and without a similar condition including this condition being imposed on the subsequent purchaser.

A CIP catalogue record for this book is available from the British Library.

ISBN: 978-1-90586-298-6

Designed and typeset by Mousemat Design Ltd
Edited by Wendy Hobson
Printed and bound in Great Britain by Bell & Bain Ltd, Glasgow

Papers used by Robinson are from well-managed forests and other responsible sources

Robinson
An imprint of
Little, Brown Book Group
Carmelite House, 50 Victoria Embankment, London EC4Y 0DZ

An Hachette UK Company
www.hachette.co.uk

www.littlebrown.co.uk

How To Books are published by Robinson, an imprint of Little, Brown Book Group. We welcome proposals from authors who have first-hand experience of their subjects. Please set out the aims of your book, its target market and its suggested contents in an email to Nikki.Read@howtobooks.co.uk

Contents

Notes and Conversions

Here are a few notes on how the recipes are presented.
- The recipes serve 4 but the portions are generous so you may find they serve more than that.
- The ingredients are listed in the order in which they are used in the recipe.
- All spoon measures are level unless otherwise stated.
- Eggs and vegetables are medium unless otherwise stated.
- Wash, peel, core and deseed, if necessary, fresh produce before use. If you prefer a hotter dish, leave chillis unseeded.
- Can and packet sizes are approximate as they vary from brand to brand.
- Preheat the oven and cook on the shelf just above the centre unless otherwise stated (this isn't necessary in a fan oven where the heat is similar throughout the oven).
- Preheat the grill and cook food about 5cm from the heat source unless otherwise stated.
- Seasoning is very much a matter of personal taste. Taste the food as you cook and adjust to suit your own palate.
- I have included some of my favourite flavour combinations as serving suggestions.

Conversion charts

Those who prefer imperial measures can use these conversions (they are approximate for ease of use).

Cup measures are convenient for things like rice or couscous. You can use American cup measuring sets, just an ordinary cup or a measuring jug. A cup is 250ml, or whatever weight fits into the space (so a cup of sugar is 225g whereas a cup of flour is 100g).

OVEN TEMPERATURES										
110ºC	120ºC	140ºC	150ºC	160ºC	180ºC	190ºC	200ºC	220ºC	230ºC	240ºC
225ºF	250ºF	275ºF	300ºF	325ºF	350ºF	375ºF	400ºF	425ºF	450ºF	475ºF
gas ¼	gas ½	gas 1	gas 2	gas 3	gas 4	gas 5	gas 6	gas 7	gas 8	gas 9

WEIGHT											
25g	50g	75g	100g	150g	175g	200g	225g	250g	300g	350g	450g
1oz	2oz	3oz	4oz	5oz	6oz	7oz	8oz	9oz	10oz	12oz	1lb

MEASUREMENTS											
5mm	5cm	10cm	13cm	15cm	18cm	20cm	25cm	30cm	35cm	40cm	45cm
¼in	2 in	4 in	5 in	6 in	7 in	8 in	10 in	12 in	14 in	16 in	18 in

LIQUID MEASURE											
5ml	15ml	50ml	60ml	75ml	100ml	125ml	150ml	200ml	300ml	450ml	600ml
1 tsp	1 tbls	2 fl oz	2½fl oz	3 fl oz	4 fl oz	4½ fl oz	5 fl oz	7 fl oz	½ pt	¾ pt	1 pt
1tsp	1 tbls	3 tbls	¼ cup	⅓ cup	Scant ½ cup	½ cup	⅔ cup	Scant 1 cup	1¼ cups	1¼ cups	2¼ cups

Introduction to Lebanese Hospitality and Culture

I was born in the Shouf mountains in a village called Gharifeh, south-east of Beirut. The Shouf is a beautiful part of Lebanon. Every family there owns their own land, where ancient olive trees grow. The people don't buy olives or olive oil but produce their own from their own trees; for the majority of people it used to be their major source of income.

My parents moved to Beirut with five young children where we could go to reasonable schools. But we couldn't wait for the school holidays so we could go up to the mountains and enjoy the freedom of the country wilderness – that was the highlight of our childhood.

We loved the rural way of life, where hospitality and generosity are exceptional, and where many people still believe in growing their own vegetables, making bread, tomato purèe and burghul (cracked wheat). My aunt, at the age of 92, still makes all these things and many more. It's a way of life that still continues, as it has for centuries, and for some people it's the only way to live a healthy life. As everywhere else, however, some of the younger generation seem less keen on working the land.

The population of our village is about 8,000 people and they are all related to one another – some close, some distant – but it's just like one big extended family. Walking around the village, apart from all the greetings and hugs along the way, you smell the aroma of fig jam and quince, used for sweets, or of tomatoes being cooked outdoors in the courtyards over wood fires for making tomato purèe. You may also catch the occasional aroma of soap that some people make from their own pure olive oil, especially if they have a surplus from the previous season. This is the Lebanon of my childhood.

The author looking over her village in the Shouf mountains.

Where my love of food began

When I was asked by a friend, who was the head of an adult education centre, to teach a class in Lebanese cooking, I said I didn't think it would run as Lebanese food was not well known. However, I was persuaded to have a go and decided to call it 'Eastern Mediterranean Food' to encourage a wider audience. The response was great! The classes were very successful, the demand for places was high and the courses ran at various centres for many years. So I felt very happy with what I was doing while bringing up my family, and at the time I didn't give a second thought to putting my recipes into a book. After all, I am not a chef nor have I even ever worked in a restaurant. Apart from teaching my courses, my main experience in food is cooking for my family and friends. But cooking has always been my number one hobby.

Four generations of the Hamadeh family.

When I was a young child growing up in Beirut, I watched my mother with fascination but she would not allow me to help with the cooking as our kitchen was always too busy. Not only did she cook for our family, there were also regular visits from family who came to Beirut from the mountains (which was then the equivalent of travelling abroad now), staying for perhaps a night or two. Our house in the city was always open and welcoming to any visitors.

My very old grandmother (*Téta*) always lived with us and was unable to walk during the last five years of her life. My mother is kind and loving; she took great care of my grandmother and never left her alone. My grandmother was so lucky to have the best daughter-in-law. Grandma understood my passion for cooking and encouraged my enthusiasm. When the family had a day out, I would stay behind to look after grandma, but with her sharp sense of humour, she'd laugh because she knew I wanted to cook. 'Only on my terms, making what I fancy eating!' she'd say and, having a sweet tooth, she usually demanded something sweet, talking me through the instructions. Her favourite dish was an old country recipe for very sweet pitta bread cooked with sugar, butter and orange flower water (*mazaher*) called *hroo osboo*. That was when my cooking experience began, with joy and a lot of laughter with my brilliant grandmother, *Téta Ammon*, who made me believe that good food is a pleasure and cooking is fun.

My mother, always a mountain woman even though she moved to live in the city of Beirut, remained a great believer in cooking traditionally authentic food. She was a great cook and very resourceful with what she knew or sometimes with what was available in the house. She was not particularly adventurous and stuck with authentic and classic Lebanese recipes – and made them brilliantly. One of the dishes she cooked quite often was *Burghul ma Banadoura* (page 190) made with coarse cracked wheat and tomatoes and served with shredded cabbage salad. This was one of my favourite foods as a child and still is.

And how it continues

I have lived in and out of Lebanon for many years, but in my heart, I have strongly felt my love and passion for Lebanon and Lebanese food. I brought up my family on Lebanese food and have always loved sharing and enjoying a feast with friends. For this, the Lebanese style is perfect, as food is never served plated, but all the different dishes are placed in the centre of the table for everyone to share.

Travel has opened the doors to so many international cuisines as more and more people travel and experience the taste of different flavours from all round the world. Most ingredients are now readily available in supermarkets, and even unusual ingredients can be found in delicatessens or specialised shops, or ordered online. In Lebanese cooking, the ingredients are mostly basic and so are easy to find in most shops.

I can simply describe Lebanese food as:

tasty

healthy

fresh

economical

The style of cooking is creative and such great fun. It's perfect for enjoying relaxing dinner parties and special occasions as you can prepare and cook most dishes in advance, thus avoiding any last-minute stress.

Another very important point is that children love the flavours and the food is not spicy. Most dishes contain lots of vegetables so it's great way to see children enjoying eating vegetables. Having brought up five children and always had young guests for dinner after school, they always requested Lebanese food.

Lebanese hospitality and culture

In spite of the political instability, the Lebanese are a fun-loving nation. Their love for Lebanon has remained throughout the troubled times, and they continue to enjoy what our country has to offer: the beauty of nature, a great climate and good food. Throughout the Middle East, the Lebanese have the reputation of enjoying life to the full and taking every opportunity to do so. Eating is a big part of that enjoyment. Food is the main focus on every occasion and it's socially important to gather round the table to share and enjoy delicious food.

The Lebanese are extremely hospitable and loving people, and this is easily demonstrated with food. When a guest comes to your house, even if they are unexpected, they must be offered something to eat. If the guest refuses, they will be offered food again at regular intervals throughout the visit. The most useful thing you can learn is not to visit a Lebanese home with a full stomach because you can offend the Lebanese by refusing to eat or drink while visiting their home. Also a Lebanese hostess will consider she has not provided enough food if everything is eaten, so they always prepare extra dishes or a larger quantity than is needed. After living in the UK for many years, I still feel uncomfortable if all the food is eaten and think people might not have had enough.

When you are invited for lunch or dinner, forget about portion control. If you plate is empty, your host will keep adding more food onto your plate, thinking that you may not have had enough. The tip is never clear your plate, which proves that you are really full and can't finish what you already have. When my English husband visited Lebanon for the first time, I made sure he knew about these rules of etiquette!

Everyday cooking in Lebanon is relaxed and works by looking and tasting – I rarely weigh and measure ingredients. But for this book, I have carefully worked out the right measurements so that the end result in your kitchen is exactly how my food comes out, which is the original way of real authentic Lebanese food.

Without the great support and enthusiasm of my husband and all my children, I would never have had the courage to write this book – thanks everyone. But, with their encouragement, I feel so excited about not only sharing my favourite recipes but also being able to express my passion for Lebanon and Lebanese food. With recipes from Mount Lebanon and down along the Mediterranean coastal strip, from south to north, in this book I will share with you the wonderful tradition of Lebanese food, authentic dishes that I am sure you will enjoy as much as I do.

Lunch arrives from the garden. All meals are accompanied by a dish of fresh vegetables.

The Cedar tree is Lebanon's heritage.

CHAPTER 1
What is Lebanese Food?

The cuisine of Lebanon has evolved throughout the centuries, influenced by the climate, the agriculture, and by a number of invasions and outside influences. One of the biggest of those was the Ottomans, which is why Lebanese food is so close to Turkish cuisine, although the Lebanese way of cooking was significantly refined by the occupation of the French.

The Lebanese eat a huge amount of vegetables and pulses, especially in the mountains where meat is not always available. This is because this depends on the local butcher, who slaughters the animal and sells the meat on the same day. When there is no meat, people cook vegetarian food – which is never a problem as there is such a huge variety of vegetarian recipes that are full of delicate combination of flavours. Pulses are enjoyed as main dishes, dips and soup. Raw vegetables – such as lettuce, whole small cucumbers, tomatoes, spring onions and green chillies – are often presented on the table to be eaten on the side with whatever you are having. Pickled vegetables are also very popular, including turnips, aubergines, cucumbers and chillies.

Nobody goes walking without a bag for foraging as there is always something edible to be found. In winter and spring, country people often go out into the wild to pick natural wild vegetables and herbs – such as wild mint and thyme (*zaatar*), leeks and asparagus, which is then chopped and fried with eggs and olive oil to make an omelette. There is also a variety of greens that are used in salads or as pastry fillings, made in the same way as Spinach Triangles (page 54). Wild fennel is also used in omelettes.

Maza – Starters

Although we often translate this as 'starters', it is really more than that. *Maza* is the main ritual of sharing a large number of dishes, especially when meeting with friends in restaurants. Like the Spanish *tapas*, everyone enjoys sharing small quantities of lots of varied and interesting dishes. It usually starts with a cold *maza* followed by hot dishes.

This is followed by a substantial main course, with side dishes, all arranged in the centre for people to help themselves. The Lebanese usually finish the meal with fresh fruit and coffee. Sweets are very popular but eaten at different times rather than as part of the meal.

Zeit – Olive oil

Olive oil has the starring role in Lebanese cuisine. In rural towns and villages, people take pride in the quality and flavour of their oil. Olive oil is not only used for cooking, it is also often drizzled on various dishes like hummus, *mtabal*, raw meat dishes, cheeses and tomatoes or even just for dipping your bread in. Therefore a bottle of olive oil is always present on every dining table. When eating out in a restaurant, my mother always carried a small bottle of her own oil to pour on her food because she classed commercial oil as second class and not to be trusted.

Villagers collecting olives.

Olives are harvested in Lebanon between October and December. The first harvests picks the olives while they are still green, but when they are left on the trees till December, the olives ripen and turn black, which makes the oil taste richer.

Every village has its own olive press where people take their olives, sitting and waiting for their turn, then staying and watching until the oil is ready to take home. It's a seasonal ritual and sociable time of the year. When you walk in the village at that time of the year, you can only smell that special aroma of olives coming from the press. Traditionally the very first stream of oil that comes out is kept separate and taken home for supper where all the family share the bread soaked in this oil, such as *bainy*, split pitta bread dipped in oil, pomegranate seeds, and whole onions roasted over wood-burning stoves.

Drinks

Arak is the Lebanese national drink, which is made of grapes and aniseed. It goes so well with Lebanese food as it complements the lemony dishes. Commercial arak is 40 per cent alcohol and is usually diluted with two-thirds water or half arak to half water. It is always served with added ice in a small glass.

Most country people grow vines and have a huge amount of grapes later in the summer.

Many distil their own arak or use a local distiller, who will distil the arak three times for the best results. People take real pride in their arak, which is much stronger than the commercial equivalent and usually has more flavour. I am a big fan of home-distilled arak and I always choose to drink it with Lebanese food.

Lebanon claims to be the oldest site in the world for producing wine. Just about all the major wine-making grapes are grown in the Bekaa Valley, which has 300 days a year of bright sunshine. Wine production in Lebanon was started 5,000 years ago when the Phoenicians settled in Lebanon and were known for having the knowledge to produce the best wine. It was then continued by the Romans.

Most of the wine produced in Lebanon is exported round the world, mainly where the Lebanese have settled. There are many wineries producing a good range of wines. Chateau Muzar, for example, is internationally regarded as a top wine.

In Lebanon itself, people tend to drink wine only in the winter months because they believe that wine heats the body too much. I find it so amusing that when I am drinking wine in the summer with Lebanese friends, they ask me how I can tolerate it in the heat.

The Mouneh – the Food to Store
Mouneh is what people make during the summer and autumn to store for the winter months, and much of this includes simply storing ingredients that are often used in Lebanese cuisine

and will last till the following summer. Other stored items involve lots more preparation and I've detailed the main ones that are made in my village.

Burghul

Burghul, or cracked wheat, is used in many recipes, such as in the national dish, *kebbeh*, and in the national salad, *tabouleh*, which is always served as a starter to any meal. It is also served with some meals instead of rice.

Most families buy their wheat in large quantities and cook it by boiling the wheat until soft, then spreading it out on sheets of cloth in the sun for several days. When the wheat is dry, it is taken to a mill to be crushed and turned into *burghal*. *Burghul* can be coarse or fine. The fine variety is always used for *kebeh* and *tabouleh* but other dishes use the coarser type.

Fruit syrups

A great deal of fruit juices are prepared and turned into syrupy concentrates. These are drunk diluted with water. Mulberry juice is the most popular fruit drink.

Jams

The late-summer fruits of quince and figs are made into thick jams full of chunky pieces and are served after a meal for a sweet taste instead of a desert. Both of these fruits carry a wonderful aroma in the air while cooking.

Pickles

Pickles are very popular in Lebanon and they are served to complement many dishes, or even to eat on their own. Street venders sell small bowls of pickles to eat while walking along. Chunky pickled cabbage leaves, turnips and tiny cucumbers, and pickled baby aubergines filled with chopped garlic, chopped walnuts and topped with olive oil.

Sumac

Sumac is a herb which has a strong lemony flavour and is used in various dishes. The berries are picked in the wild in summer when they are ripe, then dried and ground before storing. *Sumac* is also bought commercially. It is worth buying a large bag of *sumac* if you get it online or from a specialist shop as it will be more economical and keeps for almost two years.

Tomato purèe

During summer, most villagers make enough tomato purèe to last through the winter. Tens of kilos of tomatoes are squeezed and sieved, leaving behind the seeds and skin. This is mostly done in huge pots over wood fires and it takes a long time to cook. After a while, salt is

Sumac is used extensively in Lebanese cooking.

added, and the tomatoes are stirred frequently until concentrated and thick before storing in jars as a thick paste.

Zaatar

Wild thyme, *zaatar*, is picked in the summer, left to dry, then coarsely ground and mixed with ground *sumac*, roasted sesame seeds and salt, a mixture also known as *zaatar*. This is mixed with olive oil and either spread on bread or on thinly flattened dough like thin pizzas and baked in a hot oven.

Basic Ingredients

This collection of ingredients forms the basis of Lebanese cooking.

Aubergines

Aubergines, *batingan*, are very popular and there is an endless variety of dishes made with aubergines. When I was growing up, my mother would go to the vegetable market (*souk*) in Beirut and always came back with huge sack of firm, shiny aubergines – just how they should be when you buy them. She would have bought them at a bargain price, so we had them every day in one way or another. I never complained because I always loved aubergines as a child and still do.

Cinnamon

This is the most commonly used spice in Lebanese cooking, mainly with red meat recipes. Westerners tend to associate cinnamon with sweet desserts, so many people find it strange to have cinnamon in savoury dishes, although cinnamon is, in fact, often used in curry because meat and cinnamon are very compatible ingredients. I hope the idea of cinnamon with meat and chicken dishes doesn't put you off and you'll give it a try.

Cumin

Cumin is used in certain dishes, giving an earthy and warming flavour.

Coriander

Fresh coriander is a popular herb used to enhance the flavour in some dishes

Flatleaf parsley

Parsley is used both as a vegetable and as a garnish. It is bought in large bunches, especially for making *tabouleh*, which requires a large amount of parsley.

Cinnamon bark and ground cinnamon.

Garlic

Do not be alarmed by the quantity of garlic used in some recipes, in which a whole bulb or more might be included. You will soon experience how the flavour softens and blends with the other ingredients as it cooks to contribute to a wonderful flavour.

Lemons

Lemons are also a major ingredient bought by the kilo and used generously. If you find the flavour of some dishes too sharp, you can always use fewer lemons.

Mint

Mint is commonly used, either with salads, in cooking or it is often served on the side and eaten with some food to complement it.

Olives

Olives must be present on every dining table. Unlike other cultures, where they serve olives as an aperitif before a meal, the Lebanese end their meal with bread and a few olives. If you happen to forget to put olives on the table, your guests will ask for some olives at the end of the meal.

Onions

Onions are used in most dishes and sometimes in large quantities. When buying onions, feel each one because firm onions keep for longer. When cooking, the onions are usually fried first for about 10 minutes until they are softened and lightly browned, or 15–20 minutes to brown and crisp.

Rice

Rice is a main source of carbohydrate and is always served with stews, fish and chicken dishes.

Flat or pitta bread

Bread is very important to the Lebanese and pitta bread, *khibez*, is the most popular. Apart from being

Tabouleh, Parsley and Mint salad is a national salad and is a must on every Lebanese table.

Garlic bulbs piled up for sale.

Lemons are used generously in Lebanese cooking.

Dried mint is used as well as fresh mint.

the other main source of carbohydrates, we have bread with most food, especially dips, which are normally scooped up with bread. Try making your own for truly authentic results (page 230).

Tomatoes

Tomatoes are used in large quantities in both salads and cooked in all kinds of dishes. So many dishes are cooked with fresh tomatoes or include a tomato purèe as a basic sauce. Try keeping tomatoes out of the fridge as the flavour improves when they are kept at room temperature.

Tahini

Tahini is a creamy sauce made from sesame seeds. It is always served with fish, whether fried or baked. It is also used in making dips such as Hummus (page 26) and Smoky Aubergine Dip or *Baba Ghannouj* (page 24). Some old-fashioned dishes are cooked in tahini sauce instead of tomato, which makes them quite heavy.

   Tahini is available in most supermarkets or in health shops. Always make sure that you pick the light-coloured tahini and not the dark variety.

CHAPTER 2
Starters
Maza

Serving *maza*, at the beginning of the meal, is a social event where you share a huge variety of different dishes with family and friends. In traditional Lebanese restaurants, friends meet and spend four or five hours over a meal and may have around 20 to 30 different dishes of hot and cold food from which to choose.

The *maza* comprises an almost endless variety of starters, including dips, vegetables, cheeses and raw meat dishes. The latter are usually prepared with very fresh lamb and include raw *kebbeh*, *kafta* or just pure ground lean meat served with various herbs and spices on the side. These dishes are always accompanied by a generous quantity of flat bread (*khibez*), used to scoop the food with from the different dishes. *Arak*, the Lebanese national drink, is usually served with maza. The first dish is usually tabouleh, and diners move slowly on from there. There is never any hurry, and no attempt to get a bit of everything on your plate before you start.

In Lebanese restaurants, you never order a main dish at the beginning of the meal, but instead you order after you've had the maza. It is quite common for people to decide not to have a main course after eating all the maza dishes.

At home, we don't go to the extent of preparing that number of maza dishes, but even if you prepare a small variety of maza dishes to share, it makes a dinner party very special. In this chapter, you'll find the most popular Lebanese maza dishes.

The *Maza* table shown in the photo oposite was prepared for me at Draj al Tahoun restaurant in Jounieh, Lebanon.

Smoky Aubergine Dip

Mtabal or Baba Ghanouj

This aubergine dip has a unique smoky flavour. It is very popular and always served with any selection of *maza*. If you prefer it without the smoky taste, just bake the aubergine in the oven instead of cooking it over a direct flame.

SERVES 4

2 medium aubergines
Juice of 1 lemon
2 tbsp tahini
$^1/_2$ tsp salt
2 garlic cloves, crushed
1 tbsp water

To garnish
Olive oil, for drizzling
Chopped fresh mint
Pomegranate seeds
A few olives, sliced radishes,
   chopped fresh parsley
   (optional)

Serving suggestion
Pitta Bread (page 230) or
   other flatbread

Preparation time: 10 minutes
Cooking time: 1$^1/_4$ hours

• Roast the aubergines on your gas burner by resting them directly on the flame, occasionally turning them over and on to the top and bottom for about 30 minutes until the skin is burnt and crispy and you can feel the centre is very soft.

• If you choose to bake them, it is essential to prick the aubergines before putting them in the oven, as they can occasionally explode. For this method, preheat the oven to 200°C/Gas 6. Place the aubergines in a baking tin and bake in the oven for about 40 minutes.

• Allow the aubergines to cool before removing the skin and gently rinsing under the cold tap to remove any black bits.

• Mash aubergines with a fork or potato masher, add the lemon juice and mix well to prevent the aubergines from discolouring.

• Add the tahini, salt, garlic and water, and mix well.

• Spoon into a serving dish, drizzle with a little olive oil and garnish with mint and pomegranate seeds. You could also garnish with parsley, a few olives or sliced radishes; it's a personal choice.

Chickpeas with Tahini

Hummus Mtabal

Hummus has become so popular in the West that it is readily available in almost every corner shop to serve as a dip or a starter. Like the Smoky Aubergine Dip (page 24), hummus is always included on the maza table, and is also delicious with any barbecued meat. Once you've made it at home you will realise how quick and simple it is to make. Use light tahini, not whole, which is dark in colour.

SERVES 4

250g cooked chickpeas or
    105g dried chickpeas
1 tsp bicarbonate of soda if
    using dried chickpeas
130ml light tahini
2 garlic cloves, crushed
50ml lemon juice (1 large,
    juicy lemon)
1 tsp salt
60ml cold water

To garnish
Chopped fresh parsley
Sliced red pepper
A few radishes, halved
    (optional)
A little olive oil (optional)

Serving suggestion
Pitta Bread (page 230)

Preparation time: 20 minutes
    with cooked chickpeas
Cooking time: 1½ hours,
    plus soaking, if using dried
    chickpeas

- If you are using dried chickpeas, soak them overnight in water with the bicarbonate of soda.

- Drain, rinse, then place in a saucepan and cover with fresh water. Bring to the boil, cover and simmer for about 1–1½ hours until the chickpeas are very tender and soft. (Don't add salt during cooking or they will toughen.) Drain.

- For a quicker option, use tinned chickpeas. If using tinned chickpeas, I prefer to drain the water from the tin and boil the chickpeas in fresh water for a few minutes, then drain.

- Mash the chickpeas; I use a hand blender as it gives a smoother result.

- Mix in the tahini, garlic, lemon juice and salt. At this stage, the hummus will look thick and dry, so start to add the cold water little by little, blending in the mixture until it becomes smooth and creamy. Taste and adjust the salt and lemon juice to taste.

- Spoon onto a serving dish and garnish with parsley, radishes, red pepper or whatever you prefer. Drizzle with olive oil, if liked.

Cook's tip
- I often make a larger quantity and keep it in the fridge to serve for several days. It is also suitable for freezing.

Yoghurt Cream Cheese
Labneh

Labneh is a concentrated yoghurt dip. It is popular throughout the Middle East and mostly eaten at breakfast, drizzled with a little olive oil on top. It is also served with *maza* with a variety of ingredients added to it. You will need a muslin bag or any absorbent cloth to cover a fine sieve.

SERVES 4

1 litre plain yoghurt
½ tsp salt
Drizzle of olive oil (optional)

To garnish
Cucumber slices
Tomatoes
Mint

Serving suggestion
Pitta Bread (page 230) or
  other flatbread

Preparation time: 5 minutes,
  plus draining

* Put the yoghurt in a bowl and stir in the salt until dissolved.

* Place a cloth bag or muslin cloth over a sieve and pour in the yoghurt.

* Leave the yoghurt to drain for about 5 hours. It becomes as thick as whipped cream.

* Remove from the bag and keep in a sealed container in the fridge.

* To serve, drizzle with olive oil, if you like.

Chilli and Mixed Peppers Dip

Fleifleh be Zeit

This tasty and simple dip is served as part of maza or as a single starter. As it is usually served cold, it will keep in your fridge for several days so you will find it convenient for tasty snacks.

SERVES 4

3 tbsp olive oil
1 red onion, finely chopped
1 green pepper, diced
1 red pepper, diced
1 yellow pepper, diced
2 green or red chillis,
  deseeded and diced
3 garlic cloves, finely
  chopped
50g fresh parsley, chopped
½ tsp salt

To garnish
Lemon wedges

Serving suggestion
Pitta Bread (page 230)

Preparation time: 10 minutes
Cooking time: 30 minutes

• Heat the olive oil in a pan and fry the onion gently for a few minutes to soften.

• Add the peppers, chilli and garlic, cover and fry over a low heat for 20 minutes, stirring occasionally.

• Add three-quarters of the parsley and the salt and continue to fry for another 5 minutes.

• Leave to cool.

• Sprinkle with the remaining parsley, garnish with lemon wedges and serve cold.

Crushed Nut and Chilli Dip

Mhammarah

The Lebanese are not a spicy hot food nation, but with the historic presence of Armenians in Lebanon and with the influence of their delicious hot and spicy food, the Lebanese have adapted some of the Armenian spicy dishes. I had only tasted this dish in restaurants and the recipe always varied. Chef Haisam El-Ayache made the best version I have tasted, and he kindly shared his recipe with me. Since then, I have often enjoyed it at home.

The level of chilli can be varied so everyone can enjoy this spicy, nutty dish. It is so simple to prepare and full of exciting flavours. You can serve it as a starter with toasted pitta bread or as a dip to share.

SERVES 4

20g almonds
20g hazelnuts
70g cashew
30g walnuts
5–6 water biscuits
1 red pepper
60ml olive oil
1 red chilli, deseeded
1 tsp paprika
1 tsp chilli powder
½ tsp ground cumin
½ tsp salt

Serving suggestion
Pitta Bread (page 230)

Preparation time: 25 minutes

• Put all the nuts and biscuits in a food processor and process until the texture resembles coarse breadcrumbs. Tip out of the processor.

• Blend the pepper, olive oil and chilli in the processor and add to the nuts.

• Add the paprika, chilli powder, cumin and salt, and bind together by hand.

Hummus with Meat and Pine Nuts
Hummus ma Lahme wa Snoobar

There is always a demand for hummus with maza, with barbecue, as a dip with meat or even spread in sandwiches. It is also mixed with chopped parsley to make what is called *Houmos Beiruti*. For this dish, you can prepare the hummus in advance, then quickly cook lamb and pine nuts at the last minute to serve hot. It's definitely worth trying.

SERVES 4

1 quantity Chickpeas with
  Tahini (page 26)

For the topping
50ml oil
15g pine nuts
130g lean lamb, trimmed
  and diced

Serving suggestion
Pitta Bread (page 230)

Preparation time: 10 minutes
Cooking time: 10 minutes

• Spoon the hummus into a small dish, smoothing the sides and making hollow in the middle.

• Heat the oil in a small frying pan and fry the pine nuts for a few minutes to brown, then remove from the oil using a slotted spoon.

• Add the lamb to the pan and fry over a medium-high heat for 2–3 minutes until very slightly browned. Spoon it over the hummus, then sprinkle with the pine nuts.

Tahini and Onion Dip

Tagen

This tasty and simple tahini dip is often served as part of maza spread. It is served cold and therefore can be prepared in advance.

SERVES 4

100g tahini
50ml lemon juice (one
  average lemon)
About 400ml cold water
2 tbsp olive oil
200g onions, halved and
  thinly sliced
1/2 tsp salt

To garnish
15g pine nuts
A little chopped fresh parsley
Pitta Bread (page 230)
Lemon wedges

Preparation time: 15 minutes
Cooking time: 30 minutes

• Mix the tahini and lemon juice until it becomes thick and fluffy.

• Gradually add about 300ml of the cold water and keep stirring until it becomes like thin cream without lumps. Add more water if necessary.

• Heat the oil and fry the onions for about 10 minutes to soften and lightly brown.

• Add the tahini sauce and salt to the onions and mix well. Keep stirring until it starts to boil.

• Turn the heat to low and allow to simmer for 20 minutes, stirring every few minutes.

• Now the onions should look almost mushed and blended with the thickened tahini.

• Allow to cool and spread into a small serving dish.

• Sprinkle the pine nuts over the top and garnish with chopped parsley. This dish is always served with pitta bread and lemon on the side.

Smoky Aubergine Salad
Batingan Raheb

This delightful smoky salad is simple and full of flavour. It is served with pitta bread as part of the *maza* or as a starter on its own. Pomegranates come in three different varieties: the very sweet, semi-sweet and the sharp, citrusy variety. We choose to use the semi-sweet or sharp for savoury food.

SERVES 4

2 aubergines
Juice of 1½ lemons
2 garlic cloves, crushed
½ small onion, finely
   chopped
½ tsp salt

To garnish
1 tbsp olive oil
Pomegranate seeds, the sharp
   variety (optional)
1 tomato, chopped
A little chopped fresh parsley

Serving suggestion
Pitta Bread (page 230)

Preparation time: 10 minutes
Cooking time: 30 minutes

• Roast the aubergines with the skin on for about 30 minutes over the gas flame or under a hot grill, turning them occasionally until the skin is blackened and the flesh feels soft.

• Remove from the flame and leave to cool a little. Peel off the skin; this is easier while the aubergines are still fairly hot. Rinse under cold water to wash off any bits of skin.

• Discard the top and chop the flesh with a knife. Add the lemon juice. This will stop the aubergines from turning brown, especially if you are going to add the dressing later before serving.

• Add the garlic, onion and salt, then mix everything together.

• Spoon onto a serving plate, drizzle with the olive oil and sprinkle with the pomegranate seeds, if using. Spoon the tomato and parsley on the side to mix with the aubergine when serving.

Labneh Cheese with Peppers and Olives
Labneh ma Khudra

Labneh – yoghurt cream cheese – is very popular and mainly consumed with breakfast. It's a food that we always have in the fridge, which makes for an easy snack spread in a wrap with any salad or by itself with or without olive oil.

SERVES 4

1 small red pepper, diced
6 tbsp Yoghurt Cream Cheese
  (page 28)
1 garlic clove, crushed
2 spring onions, chopped
12 green or black olives,
  stoned and chopped
$\frac{1}{2}$ tsp dried mint
$\frac{1}{4}$ tsp salt
A little olive oil
Serving suggestion
Toasted Pitta Bread (page
  230)

Preparation time: 10 minutes

• Reserve one-third of the pepper for garnish, then simply mix together all the remaining ingredients except the oil.

• Transfer to a small serving dish, drizzle with the oil and garnish with the reserved pepper.

Cook's tip
• To make it even simpler, you can just add garlic and mint to the *labneh*, then drizzle with a little olive oil.

Minced Beef or Lamb Pastry Crescents

Sambousak

Sambousak is often served with a selection of other pastries like Spinach Triangles (page 54), Feta Cheese Pasties (page 44) and Kebbeh Balls (page 48). With a little patience, they are easy to make and very tasty.

SERVES 4

For the pastry
200g plain flour, plus extra
  for rolling out
½ tsp salt
3 tbsp olive oil
About 100ml water

For the filling
2–4 tbsp olive oil
20g pine nuts
1 large onion, chopped
  (about 200g)
200g minced beef or lamb
½ tsp ground cinnamon
Salt and freshly ground black
  pepper

Preparation time: 1½ hours
Cooking time: 30 minutes

• Mix the flour and salt, then rub in the olive oil.

• Add enough of the water little by little, blending into the flour until you form a smooth dough. Wrap in clingfilm and leave to rest in the fridge while preparing the filling.

• Heat 2 tbsp of the oil and fry the pine nuts over a low heat for a few minutes to brown, then remove from the pan using a slotted spoon.

• Add the onion to the pan and fry for a few minutes to brown lightly, then add the meat and fry together with the onion, stirring until browned.

• Finally, stir in the cinnamon and pine nuts and season to taste with salt and pepper. Mix well.

• Roll the pastry out thinly on a lightly floured surface and cut into circles about 8cm in diameter.

• Place 1 tsp of the filling on half of each circle, then fold the other half over the top. Squeeze the edges firmly to stick. Starting from one corner, pinch the edge and twist all round to the other corner to create a decorative edge.

• Heat a little more oil in a frying pan and fry the sambousak for about 5–10 minutes over a medium heat to brown, turning once. You may need to do this in batches so keep them warm while you fry the remainder.

Cook's tip
• I sometimes make a large quantity and freeze them before cooking. Then when you need them, you can simply fry them in hot oil straight out of the freezer.

Feta Cheese Pasties

Sambousak Jibneh

These always go down a treat. They are simple to make and delicious to serve as starter or a canapé.

SERVES 4

1 quantity *Sambousak* pastry
   (page 42)
250g feta cheese
1 onion, chopped
25g fresh parsley, chopped
Olive oil, for deep-frying

Preparation time: 1 hours
Cooking time: 30 minutes

• Make the pastry as on page 42 and leave to rest.

• Crumble the cheese with the tips of your fingers, then gently mix in the chopped onions and chopped parsley, pressing them gently so they hold together.

• Roll out the pastry on a lightly floured surface and cut into 8cm circles.

• Place 1 tsp of the filling on each circle, fold over, press the edges together and make a pattern with the end of a fork.

• Heat the deep-frying oil in a heavy-based pan until very hot, and deep-fry the sambousak, in batches if necessary, for about 5–10 minutes until browned. Serve hot.

Cook's tip
• These are perfect for freezing and always handy to have for a tasty starter or as a snack with drinks. Just open-freeze the uncooked pasties, then seal them in a freezer container or bag. Fry them straight from freezer.

Mince and Chickpea Pasties

Fatayer Hummus

When I recently went to my regular bakery in the village to buy bread, I saw little pasties that the baker had just made. They looked different from his usual pasties so I asked what was in them and he told me that they were lamb and chickpea pasties. Needless to say, I tried them and liked them, not because it was something new but because tasting this very old-fashion recipe that is rarely made now brought back childhood memories.

SERVES 4

For the dough
300g plain flour, plus extra
    for rolling out
1 tsp instant dried yeast
1/2 tsp salt
3 tbsp oil
About 150ml water

For the filling
220g dried chickpeas,
    soaked
50ml oil
230g onions, chopped
130g minced lamb
2 tsp ground cumin
1/2 tsp ground cinnamon
1/2 tsp black pepper
1/2 tsp salt

Preparation time: 1 1/2–2
    hours
Cooking time: 30 minutes

• Mix the flour, yeast and salt. Gradually add the oil and enough water to mix to a smooth dough. Knead thoroughly.

• Place the dough in an oiled bowl, cover with a damp tea towel and leave in a warm place until doubled in size.

• Drain the chickpeas, then process in a food processor.

• Heat the oil in a frying pan and fry the onions until they begin to brown.

• Add the mince and continue to fry, stirring, until the meat is browned.

• Add the chickpeas and stir with the meat for few minutes.

• Add the cumin, cinnamon, pepper and salt and keep stirring for another 2 minutes. Remove from the heat and set aside.

• Preheat the oven to 220°C/Gas 7 and heat a baking tray in the oven.

• Divide the dough into 2 balls and roll out on a floured surface. Cut into circles, choosing whatever size you prefer for your pasties.

• Generously place some of the filling on one half of the circle, then fold the other half over the filling and seal the edges with a fork.

• Arrange the pies on the prepared baking tray, leaving space between and bake for 20 minutes until cooked through and golden brown.

Cook's tip
• You may need to prepare and cook them in batches.

Kebbeh Balls

Kebbeh Mehshiyeh

As *kebbeh* is the most Lebanese national dish, it is always served in one way or another. These *kebbeh* balls are always served with maza starters, or as canapè when made bite size. It's really worth having a go at making them.

MAKES 15–20

Use the same ingredients for the *kebbeh* and the filling as in the Kebbeh with Bulgur Wheat, page 124, but only half the quantity.

Preparation time: 1¼ hours
Cooking time: 30 minutes

• For making the *kebbeh* and the filling, follow the recipe on page 124.

• Divide the *kebbeh* into small balls about the size of a golf ball and hold between your thumb and fingers so you can make it hollow with your index finger. You may need to wet your hands sometimes when the *kebbeh* starts to stick on your hands.

• Fill with 1 tsp of the meat filling, then close and seal the top end of it.

• Make sure there are no cracks. If there are, just smooth them over with your finger. If the balls are cracked, they will burst while frying.

• Heat the oil in a deep pan until very hot. Turn the heat down a little, then gently slide each *kebbeh* ball into the pan, making sure they are not touching. Fry for about 10 minutes until dark brown.

• Remove from the heat and fry the remaining balls in the same way. Serve hot.

Kafta and Tahini Toasties

Arayes

These rustic-looking and extremely simple toasties are exceptionally delicious served as snacks or starter.

SERVES 4

400g minced lamb
1 onion, finely chopped
30g fresh parsley, finely
   chopped
1/4 tsp ground cinnamon
1/2 tsp salt
Freshly ground black pepper
6 Lebanese bread loaves or
   Pitta Bread (page 230)
Tahini Sauce (page 232)

Preparation time: 20 minutes
Cooking time: 10–15
   minutes

• Preheat the oven to 200°C/Gas 6.

• Mix the minced lamb with the onion, parsley, cinnamon, salt and pepper. Knead the mixture until it becomes well combined.

• Cut the bread loaves into quarters and spread some of the *kafta* meat inside each piece.

• Drizzle each one with 2 tsp tahini sauce.

• Bake in the oven for 10–15 minutes until cooked through and crisp. Serve hot.

Feta Cheese and Filo Slices
Rakakat Jibneh

This recipe is so simple and tasty, and great for snacks or starters. While writing this book I have become a big fan of filo pastry. It is so easy to use and you can just about wrap anything in it. Just remember not to let it dry out while you are working; if necessary, cover it with a damp tea towel.

270g packet of filo pastry
80g butter, melted
200g feta cheese
80g onion, finely chopped
20g fresh parsley, chopped
Freshly ground black pepper
    to taste

Preparation time: 30 minutes
Cooking time: 45 minutes

- Preheat the oven to 180°C/Gas 4.

- Unwrap the filo and cut the sheets through into halves.

- Brush the base of a 25cm square baking tin with a little of the melted butter and place first sheet of filo in the base of the tin.

- Brush with a little more, then place another sheet on top. Repeat procedure until you have used half of the filo.

- With your fingers, crumble the cheese and mix with onion, parsley and black pepper to taste. Spread evenly over the filo pastry.

- As before, complete layering the remaining filo over the cheese, brushing each sheet with butter.

- With a sharp knife, cut the pastry all through to the bottom into small squares.

- Bake in the oven for 45 minutes when it should be a golden colour.

- Cut and separate the squares to place on a serving plate and serve hot.

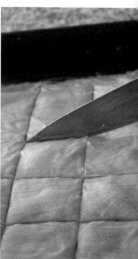

Spinach Triangles
Fatayer Sabanekh

Fatayer is one of the popular snacks that you can buy from any bakery, but they are also often made at home. They can be made any size, but for buffets, canapés and *maza* they are usually made quite small (so you eat them in two or three bites). This picture was taken at the bakery where I go to collect bread and my order of spinach pies. The baker used his dough and the filling that I prepared, then baked them ready to go.

SERVES 4

For the dough
400g wholemeal or white
   bread flour or a mixture,
   plus extra for rolling out
1 sachet instant dry yeast
$\frac{1}{2}$ tsp salt
About 200ml warm water

For the filling
400g chopped fresh spinach
1 large onion, chopped
2 tsp sumac or the juice of 1
   extra lemon
Juice of 1 lemon
3 tbsp olive oil
$\frac{1}{2}$ tsp salt

Preparation time: $1\frac{1}{2}$–2
   hours, plus rising
Cooking time: 25 minutes

• In a bowl, mix the flour, yeast and salt, then gradually add enough of the warm water to form a soft but not sticky dough. Knead for a couple of minutes until smooth and elastic, then roll it into a ball. Cover and leave in a warm place for a couple of hours to double its size.

• Prepare the filling by mixing the spinach with all remaining filling ingredients. Place the filling in a colander over a bowl so it will drain out any excess fluid while you prepare the dough. If the filling is too wet, it will stop the dough edges from sticking and sealing the filling inside the triangle shape.

• Knead the dough again for a few minutes. Take a chunk of the dough and roll it out on a lightly floured surface to 2–3mm thick, then cut it into neat circles with a round pastry cutter or a cup, depending on the size you want. Roll out and cut the remaining circles.

• Preheat the oven to 230°C/Gas 8 and place a baking tray in the oven to heat.

• Place a spoonful of the drained filling on a circle of dough, then fold over the edges to form a triangle and press the edges together to seal.

• Place the *fatayer* on the heated oven tray, allowing little space between them as they expand while baking.

• Bake in the oven for about 20 minutes until they are slightly golden and crisp.

• Leave to cool on a wire rack before serving.

Cook's tip
• *Fatayer* can be frozen before or after baking.

Whitebait

Samak Bezri

This seasonal fish is only caught between May and September. During the season, whitebait is frequently served fried in Lebanon, with a bowl of tahini sauce and lot of lemons for squeezing.

SERVES 4

500g whitebait
1 tsp salt
40g plain flour
Oil, for deep-frying

To garnish
2 lemons, cut into wedges

Serving suggestion
Simple Tahini Sauce (page 232)
Pitta Bread (page 230)

Preparation time: 15 minutes
Cooking time: 20 minutes

• Gut the fish but keep the heads on, or buy them ready prepared. Wash thoroughly, drain, then sprinkle with 1 tsp of salt and set aside for 1 hour before frying

• Heat the oil in a deep pan for frying.

• Take a handful of fish and toss in the flour, shaking off any excess before they go in the pan.

• Lower them into the hot oil for 5–10 minutes, turning the fish only once or twice, allow to turn slightly crispy, then lift out of the oil using a slotted spoon and drain on kitchen paper. Keep them warm while you fry the remaining fish.

• Garnish with lemon wedges and serve hot.

Chicken Livers with Garlic and Coriander
Kasabet Djaj

Chicken liver is often a part of the hot maza that is usually served after the cold starters. It is extremely delicious and simple in all the different ways it is prepared.

SERVES 4

2 tbsp oil
500g fresh chicken livers, diced
3 garlic cloves, crushed
30g chopped fresh coriander
Juice ½ lemon
½ tsp salt
¼ tsp freshly ground black pepper

To garnish
Lemon wedges

Preparation time: 10 minutes
Cooking time: 10 minutes

• Heat the oil in a frying pan and fry the diced liver on a high heat for about 10 minutes, turning occasionally until it becomes almost brown.

• Add the crushed garlic and two-thirds of the chopped coriander and stir for 2 more minutes.

• Add the lemon juice, salt and pepper, stir in, then remove from the heat.

• Sprinkle remaining coriander on the top and serve immediately with extra lemon on the side.

Cook's tips
• This dish takes only 10 minutes to prepare. Make sure you don't overcook it as liver becomes dry if overcooked.

• You can simply fry the liver with a squeeze of lemon if you prefer.

• Sometimes this is served with 1 tbsp pomegranate molasses stirred in instead of the lemon juice.

Citrus Chicken Wings

Jawaneh Djaj

Chicken wings are often served as a starter as they make a great part of a spread and many people prefer chicken wings to any other part of the chicken. This recipe is quick, simple and full of flavour.

SERVES 4

10–12 chicken wings
2 tbsp olive oil
4–5 garlic cloves, finely chopped
30g fresh coriander, chopped
Juice of 1 lemon
$1/2$ tsp salt

Preparation time: 10 minutes
Cooking time: 40 minutes

• Trim the wings by cutting off the pointy part at the end and any excess skin, then cut into halves at the joint.

• Heat the oil and fry the wings over a high heat for about 5 minutes until brown on all sides.

• Turn the heat to very low, cover the pan and continue to cook for about 20 minutes to make sure the wings are cooked through.

• Add the garlic and coriander and stir for couple of minutes.

• Finally add lemon juice and salt and simmer for 2 more minutes to get a hot glaze over the chicken pieces. Serve hot.

Potatoes with Chilli and Coriander
Batata Harrah

I am not a big fan of potatoes, but I love this recipe and could eat it every day. Although it is called Potatoes with Chilli, the chilli is optional as not everyone likes spicy food. Even without the chilli, the wonderful flavours are there. It is served in small portions if part of a maza, and can also be served with fish, chicken or meat.

SERVES 4

5 tbsp oil
500g potatoes, peeled and
 cubed
4 garlic cloves, chopped
1 chopped green chilli
 (optional)
50g fresh coriander, chopped
Salt
Juice of ½ lemon

Preparation time: 20 minutes
Cooking time: 30 minutes

• Heat the oil in a frying pan and fry the potatoes to lightly brown on all sides.

• Add the garlic, chilli, coriander and salt and fry all together for another 5 minutes, stirring occasionally.

• Add the lemon juice and serve immediately.

CHAPTER 3

Salads and Soups
Salata wa Shorba

Salads are never served as a meal in themselves, but you would always see some kind of salad on the table to be served as a refreshing side dish and to complement the main courses. Such salads include shredded cabbage, mixed green salad, tomato salad, which is always mixed with mint, and yoghurt and mint salad. Mint is a very popular ingredient in salads.

Tabouleh, the parsley salad, is a national dish and always served as a starter; small portion of tabouleh is always included with *maza*. When people invite you for a drink, you can be sure that you will get tabouleh with whatever snacks they serve. If tabouleh is missing from the table, I would feel cheated and so would every other Lebanese.

Another popular and refreshing salad I have included is *Fattoush*, pitta bread crouton salad.

Soup is never served as a starter and is never on menus in restaurants. When soup is made at home, it is served as a meal, because our soups are very filling and satisfying. There is only a small choice of Lebanese soups, with vegetables, pulses and chicken or meat. I have included the main Lebanese soups that are quite different from the usual soups that people make.

Parsley and Mint Salad
Tabouleh

This national salad is a must on every Lebanese table. It's the start of any meal, it's served as part of the *maza*, as a first course, with drinks and snacks and even as part of afternoon tea before you have cakes. My granddaughter, Yasmina, loves *tabouleh* so much, that I have to make it every day when she visits.

SERVES 4

200g fresh flatleaf parsley
  (about 2–3 bunches)
15g fresh mint
1 small onion, very finely
  chopped
Freshly ground black pepper
40g burghul (fine bulgur
  wheat)
400g tomatoes, diced into
  very small pieces
100ml olive oil
100ml lemon juice
½ tsp salt

To garnish
Lettuce leaves

Preparation time: 30 minutes

• Cut off and discard the thick parsley stalks, then chop the leaves with stems finely. Pick the mint leaves off the stalks and also chop very finely. Rinse the parsley and mint, then leave in a sieve to allow the water to drain.

• Rub a little freshly ground black pepper into the onion to stop the onion from having too strong a taste and smell.

• Now rinse the fine burghul with cold water and drain all the water immediately.

• Finally mix all the ingredients in a bowl and serve at once.

• Tabouleh is always served with lettuce leaves for scooping just as we use bread dips.

Tabouleh is the author's granddaughter Yasmina's favourite dish.

Yoghurt and Cucumber Salad
Salata Laban

Most people are familiar with this salad, which is normally served as a dip in the UK. In Lebanon it is served as a salad with food that is dry and requires moisture. As a yoghurt dressing, it also adds a fabulous flavour to certain dishes.

SERVES 4

150g cucumber, chopped
300ml plain yoghurt (whole
  or low fat)
1 garlic clove, crushed
$\frac{1}{2}$ tsp salt
1 tbsp chopped fresh mint or
  1 tsp dried mint
$\frac{1}{2}$ tbsp olive oil (optional)

Preparation time: 10 minutes

- Stir the cucumber into the yoghurt.

- Add the garlic and salt and blend well.

- Turn into a serving bowl, sprinkle with mint and drizzle with olive oil, if liked, to serve.

Green Bean Salad
Salata Loubeyeh

This salad can be served with any meat. You can use any kind of green beans depending on what is available at the time.

SERVES 4

500g green beans, trimmed
   and cut into chunks
1 garlic clove, crushed
2 tbsp lemon juice
1 tbsp olive oil
Pinch of salt
1 tbsp chopped fresh parsley

Preparation time: 10 minutes
Cooking time: 10 minutes

• Cook the beans in boiling salted water for 10 minutes until tender, then drain and rinse in cold water. Allow to cool.

• Mix together the garlic, lemon juice, olive oil and salt to make the dressing.

• Pour over the beans and toss gently to coat.

• Turn onto a serving dish and sprinkle parsley on the top to serve.

Lemony Potato Salad
Salata Batata

This potato salad goes well with various dishes, including all kinds of meat and fish. It is also served with other salads as part of a salad meal.

SERVES 4

900g potatoes, peeled and
  diced
2 garlic cloves, crushed
1 red onion, chopped
100ml lemon juice
1 tsp salt
50ml olive oil
15g chopped fresh parsley

Preparation time: 15 minutes
Cooking time: 15 minutes

- Cook the potatoes in boiling salted water for 10–15 minutes until just tender; do not overcook.

- Drain and rinse with cold water, which stops them sticking together, then leave them to cool.

- Mix together the garlic, onion, lemon juice, salt and olive oil.

- Add the parsley to the potatoes, then stir gently into the dressing.

- Serve with fish, chicken or meat.

Tahini Salad

Salata Tarator

Tahini sauce is always served when fish is on the table whether it's fried or baked. Tahini salad complements Fish with Saffron Rice (page 156) beautifully.

SERVES 4

100ml light tahini
1 garlic clove, crushed
50ml lemon juice
½ tsp salt
120ml cold water
230g tomatoes, chopped
40g fresh parsley, finely
   chopped

Preparation time: 20 minutes

- Mix together the tahini, garlic, lemon juice and salt in a bowl. The tahini will look stiff and dry.

- Gradually blend in a little of the water at a time, stirring all the time, until the tahini is smooth and free of lumps and is the thickness of double cream.

- Add the tomatoes and parsley and stir everything together.

- Serve with fish dishes.

Pitta Bread Crouton Salad
Fattoush

This is one of the most popular salads in Lebanon. Sometimes it is served as an alternative to tabouleh but it is much simpler and quicker to make, as well as being refreshing and tasty. There are no rules in making fattoush, you can simply use the ingredients you like or that are available, apart from for the toasted bread, onions and especially the mint, which must always be included. Some people only like to use lemon juice and oil for the dressing, while others use wine vinegar instead of lemon juice. You can also add a clove of crushed garlic if you like.

SERVES 4

150g cos or Iceberg lettuce, shredded
150g cucumber, chopped
1 onion or ½ a bunch of spring onions, chopped
1 green chilli, seeded and chopped (optional)
1 green, red or yellow pepper, chopped
450g tomatoes, chopped
30g fresh parsley, roughly chopped
25g mint leaves, roughly chopped
6 radishes, sliced
Handful of pomegranate seeds (if available)
2 heaped tsp ground sumac (or substitute 1 tbsp lemon juice)
Juice of 1 lemon
2–3 pitta bread
100ml olive oil
½ tsp salt

Preparation time: 30–40 minutes

• Preheat the grill or the oven to 200°C/Gas 6.

• Mix the lettuce, cucumber, onions, chilli, pepper and tomatoes in a bowl. Stir in the parsley and mint.

• Add the radishes, pomegranate seeds, if using, *sumac* and lemon juice.

• Split and cut the bread into small pieces, place on a baking tray and drizzle with olive oil. Toast under the grill or in the oven to brown.

• Sprinkle with salt, toss the ingredients together and add the croutons just before serving.

Cabbage Salad
Salata Malfoof

There is only one variety of cabbage in Lebanon; it is enormous and the leaves are very thin, tender and sweet. It is full of goodness and fibre, especially raw. There are three ways of eating cabbage in Lebanon: as stuffed cabbage leaves, in a salad or pickled. Cabbage is very popular and eaten frequently, and cabbage salad is one of the most popular salads, which strongly complements many Lebanese dishes; it is especially good with Green Lentils with Caramelised Onions (page 184) and Bulgur Wheat with Tomatoes (page 190).

SERVES 4

Juice of 1 lemon
30ml olive oil
1 garlic clove, crushed
½ tsp salt
400g tender cabbage,
  shredded

Preparation time: 15 minutes

- Blend the lemon juice, oil, garlic and salt.

- Pour over the cabbage and mix well just before serving.

- Taste and add more lemon juice as the flavour should be strongly lemony.

Vegetable and Garlic Yoghurt Salad
Fetteh Khudra

This unusual, tasty salad has always been popular with its interesting mix of ingredients. It is a great combination, easy to serve, and suitable to serve either as a starter or as a meal.

SERVES 4

3 tbsp cooking oil
2 potatoes, peeled and cut into small cubes
1 aubergine, cut into small cubes
1 small onion, very thinly sliced
2 tsp sumac
1 loaf pitta bread
½ tbsp olive oil
2 small garlic cloves
½ tsp salt
500ml yoghurt
1 cos lettuce, thinly sliced
120g cooked chickpeas
Pinch of dried mint

Preparation time: 45 minutes
Cooking time: 20 minutes

- Preheat the grill or the oven to 200°C/Gas 6.

- In a frying pan, heat the cooking oil and fry the potatoes and aubergine for about 10 minutes to brown, then remove from the oil and drain on kitchen paper.

- Rub the onion with the *sumac* and leave it aside.

- Split open the bread, cut it into small pieces, drizzle with olive oil and grill or bake in the oven for a few minutes to brown.

- Crush the garlic with the salt, then mix with the yoghurt.

- Assemble the ingredients in a glass dish by adding the lettuce first, then the onion followed by the aubergine and potatoes. Spread the chickpeas on top of the vegetables, then the pitta croutons over the top.

- Pour the garlic yoghurt over the salad and sprinkle with a pinch of dried mint. Serve as soon as this salad is assembled.

Tomato and Red Onion Salad

Salata Banadoura

An ideal combination of flavours that I couldn't resist sharing, I recommend you use ripe vine tomatoes for this salad as they are full of flavour. I like to have this salad on the side with so many dishes, and I particularly enjoy eating it with fried fish.

SERVES 4

500g vine tomatoes, halved
  and sliced
1/2 red onion, thinly sliced
10g fresh mint leaves,
  coarsley chopped
1/2 tbsp lemon juice
1 tbsp olive oil
1/2 tsp salt

Preparation time: 10 minutes

- Mix together the tomatoes, onion and mint.
- Mix the lemon juice, oil and salt.
- Add to the salad ingredients, mix well and serve.

Split Lentil Soup
Shorba Adas

This is traditional lentil soup: tasty, very filling and so easy to make with only a few ingredients. A friend of mine told me that her kids lived on this thick and filling soup during their university years. It can be varied by adding any other vegetables.

SERVES 4

300g split red lentils
75ml olive oil
280g onions, chopped
1 heaped tsp ground cumin
1 tsp salt
Juice of 1 lemon

To garnish
Diced roasted red peppers

Preparation time: 5 minutes
Cooking time: 1½ hours

• Cook the lentils in enough boiling water to cover for 30–40 minutes until they are mushy, adding more boiling water if necessary, as they absorb a lot of water. Do not add salt or they will toughen.

• Heat the oil and fry the onions over a moderate heat for about 10 minutes to become golden brown.

• Add the cumin and stir with the onions for few seconds, then add to the lentils.

• Season with salt and simmer gently for another 20 minutes.

• Stir in the lemon juice and garnish with roasted peppers.

Cook's tip
• This soup can be varied by adding chopped tomatoes, carrots or chopped red and green peppers. My favourite is with roasted peppers mixed in, saving a little to put on the top, as in the photograph.

Lemony Chicken and Vegetable Soup
Khoudra ma Djaj

Vegetable soup is usually cooked with a few cubes of lamb or beef. When I was visiting a friend in the village, she offered me this soup but with chicken instead of meat. I really enjoyed it and thought it was worth adding to the soup section as now I make it often.

SERVES 4

1 chicken breast fillet, cut into small slices
Salt
2 white turnips, peeled and coarsely chopped
2 carrots, peeled and coarsely chopped
1 onion, peeled and coarsely chopped
2 courgettes, coarsely chopped
3 tomatoes, coarsely chopped
Juice of 1 lemon
50g parsley, finely chopped

Serving suggestion
Crusty bread

Preparation time: 5 minutes
Cooking time: 1 hour

- Boil the chicken in water and a pinch of salt for about 15 minutes until cooked through.

- Add all the chopped vegetables.

- Cover the pan and allow to simmer for 30 minutes.

- Add the lemon juice and parsley and cook for a further 5 minutes.

- Taste for lemon and salt and add a bit more lemon if the soup doesn't taste lemony enough; it should be strongly lemon-flavoured.

- Grind fresh black pepper over the top.

Mixed Pulses Thick Soup
Makhloota

This country soup expresses mountain people's love for eating pulses. It takes a long time to cook every kind of pulse separately, so when people make this, they cook a large amount because it takes them a long time. Once it's cooked everyone huddles up round the fire eating the warming makhloota. But don't let this put you off because it doesn't have to take hours if you use tinned pulses. I tried it and I thought it was just as good. Why make life difficult? Use one can of each type.

SERVES 4

50ml olive oil
350g onions, coarsely
    chopped
2½ tsp ground cumin
1 tsp ground cinnamon
1 tsp freshly ground black
    pepper
250g cooked chickpeas,
    rinsed and drained
250g cooked kidney beans,
    rinsed and drained
250g cooked white beans,
    rinsed and drained
250g cooked lentils, with the
    stock
1 litre boiling water, plus
    more later
1 tsp salt
100g coarse burghul (bulgur
    wheat) preferably brown

Serving suggestion
Hot Pitta Bread (page 230)

Preparation time: 5 minutes
Cooking time: 1 hour

- Heat the oil in a large saucepan and fry the onions for a few minutes to soften.

- Add the cumin, cinnamon and pepper and keep frying for 2 minutes.

- Add all the pulses with the boiling water and the salt. Simmer gently for 20 minutes.

- Finally add burghul and cook for another 15 minutes. The soup should be thick but if you prefer it less thick, then just add little more water.

Green Lentil and Spinach Soup
Adas Bhamoud

This extremely healthy and very tasty, lemon-flavoured soup is always enjoyed by everyone, either hot or cold. Usually we use chard, which some people call silver beet, adding everything, including the stalks. In the UK, you are more likely to find chard in markets than in the supermarkets, so if you can't find silver beet or chard, then use large spinach leaves, which are just as delicious. When I make this dish I have it as a meal on its own as it is quite substantial.

SERVES 4

350g green lentils
55ml olive oil
320g onions, chopped
600g spinach or chard,
   chopped
1½ tsp salt
100ml lemon juice

Serving suggestion
Pitta Bread (page 230)

Preparation time: 5 minutes
Cooking time: 1½ hours

- Cook the lentils in boiling water for 30–50 minutes until they become soft.

- Heat the oil in a separate pan and fry onions for a few minutes until soft and beginning to brown, then add to the lentils.

- Add the chopped spinach or chard and simmer gently for a further 20 minutes.

- Now add salt and lemon juice and cook for another 10 minutes before serving.

CHAPTER 4

Meat, Poultry and Fish Main Dishes

Aklaat Louhoom Ra'eesiyeh

In this section you will find a large variety of meat dishes: dishes that are easy to prepare and suitable to cook daily for your family, as well as for entertaining, even if you are on a tight budget. The majority of the dishes in this section can be prepared or cooked in advance.

In many dishes you can vary the amount of meat you use. Vegetables are the most important ingredients and, as there are no rules, you will find that you can easily increase the proportion of vegetables or, if you prefer more meaty food, then you can make meat the dominant ingredient.

As I mentioned in the introduction, cinnamon is always used with meat, which many people who are used to using it only in sweet dishes find odd. However, cinnamon is an important ingredient and the flavour is very subtle when blended with other ingredients. You will only be convinced after trying it.

Celebration Lamb with Rice and Nuts
Ouzi

Ouzi is a centrepiece dish, always served at any special occasion such as social gatherings, dinner parties and weddings. It is perfect when you have to feed a large number of people and simple enough to make for the family any day in a smaller quantity. For a really large number of people, a whole lamb would be put on the table.

SERVES 6

2kg shoulder or leg of lamb
2 tbsp plain yoghurt
2 tsp ground cinnamon
1/2 tsp black pepper
500g long-grain rice
100ml cooking oil
100g split or flaked almonds
40g pine nuts
200g minced beef
1/2 tsp mixed spice
1/2 tsp salt

Serving suggestion
Yoghurt and Cucumber Salad
    (page 68)
Mixed green salad with
    Lebanese Salad Dressing
    (page 233)

Preparation time: 15 minutes
Cooking time: 1 1/2–2 hours

- Rub the lamb with the yoghurt, 1 tsp of the cinnamon and the pepper, then leave to marinate for few hours, if possible.

- Preheat the oven to 220°C/Gas 7.

- Put the meat in the oven for 15 minutes, then reduce the oven temperature to 160°C/Gas 3 and cook slowly for at least 2 hours until the meat is virtually falling off the bone.

- Rinse the rice well and soak in cold water for about 1 hour before cooking.

- Meanwhile, heat the oil and fry the almonds for a few minutes until browned.

- Remove from the pan using a slotted spoon and drain on kitchen paper.

- Then fry the pine nuts in the oil until browned, then remove from the oil.

- Finally, add the minced beef to the oil and fry for about 15 minutes, stirring regularly, until the grains are separate and the mince is brown and slightly crispy.

- Just as the meat is ready, drain and rinse the rice, then put in a pan, just cover with fresh hot water to 1cm above the level of the rice, and add the spices and salt.

- Stir in the mince and a small handful of the nuts into the rice, then bring to the boil and simmer for about 3 minutes until most of the water has evaporated from the top.

- Turn the heat right down, cover the pan and simmer for about 20 minutes until all the moisture has evaporated.

- Turn the rice onto a flat serving dish, place the joint or the meat pieces, if preferred, on top of the rice and spread the nuts all over the top.

Mini Lamb Pizzas

Sfeeha Baalbekeyeh

This recipe is famously known as the speciality of Baalebek, a historic town in the west of Lebanon known as the Roman Settlement, with its magnificent ruins and temples, visited by all foreign tourists. Traditionally, *sfeeha* is ordered at the butcher, who prepares the meat before passing it to the baker next door. After the baking, you settle down at a little table in the back of the butcher's shop with a big pile of *sfeeha*. Plain yoghurt is served on the side for dipping the *sfeeha* in.

MAKES ABOUT 24

For the dough
300g plain flour, plus extra
   for rolling out
1 sachet instant dried yeast
1/2 tsp salt
About 150ml warm water

For the topping
400g minced lamb
250g onions, finely chopped
1 tomato, seeded and
   chopped
1/2 tsp ground cinnamon
1/2 tsp salt
1/2 tsp freshly ground black
   pepper
Seeds of 1/2 pomegranate
   (optional)

Serving suggestion
Plain yoghurt

Preparation time: 1 hour
   plus rising
Cooking time: 15–20
   minutes

• Mix the flour with the yeast and salt, then gradually add enough water to create a smooth, non-sticky dough. Knead the dough until it becomes smooth without any flour pockets.

• Place the dough in an oiled bowl – bearing in mind that it will double its size when risen – cover with a damp towel and keep in a warm place or at just room temperature for 2 hours until doubled in size.

• Mix all the filling ingredients except the pomegranate seeds, if using, then turn into a sieve over a bowl to allow some of the juice to drain.

• Preheat the oven to maximum and place a thick, flat baking sheet or an oven tray in the oven.

• Take a piece of the dough, roll it out thinly on a lightly floured surface and cut into circles, using either a pastry cutter or a glass.

• Spread 2 tsp of the meat mixture over the dough and sprinkle with a few pomegranate seeds.

• Place the pizzas on the hot baking sheet and bake in the oven for 10–15 minutes.

• You may need to do this in batches.

Lamb and Aubergine Bake
Moutabaka

I find this dish suitable for any day of the week and all the family enjoy it. But I have also been pleased, after serving it at dinner parties, when people have said how much they enjoyed it and asked for the recipe. It is easily prepared in advance, then all you have to do is cook in the oven for 1 hour before dinner. You can use courgettes instead of aubergines if you prefer.

SERVES 4

4 aubergines, cut into 2cm
   thick slices
1 tsp salt
50ml olive oil
2 large onions, chopped
500g minced lamb or beef
1 tsp ground cinnamon
$\frac{1}{2}$ tsp freshly ground black
   pepper
600g tomatoes, sliced
100g tomato purèe diluted in
   400ml water
Oil, for frying aubergines

Serving suggestion
Plain basmati rice or
   Lebanese Rice with
   Vermicelli (page 228)

Preparation time: 10 minutes
Cooking time: 1–1$\frac{1}{2}$ hours

- Sprinkle a little salt on the aubergines and leave them for 1 hour on a sieve or kitchen paper.

- Preheat the oven to 220°C/Gas 7.

- Heat the 50ml of oil and fry the onions for a few minutes until they begin to brown.

- Add the meat and continue frying, stirring, to brown the meat.

- Add the cinnamon and pepper and keep stirring for another 2 minutes.

- In a separate pan, heat a little oil and shallow-fry the aubergines to brown on both sides.

- Arrange half the aubergines in the bottom of an ovenproof dish. Evenly spread the meat mixture over the aubergines. Cover the meat with remaining aubergines, then cover with the sliced tomatoes.

- Season the diluted tomato purèe with salt and pour over the aubergines.

- Bake in the preheated oven for 35 minutes.

Minced Lamb Kebab
Kafta Mishwi

Kafta is a mixture of mince, onions and parsley. It is one of the very popular dishes in the Middle East, which can be baked with potatoes and tomatoes, grilled or barbecued on skewers, or toasted in pitta bread. Whichever way you cook this tasty mixture, it is quick and simple.

SERVES 4

500g minced lamb or beef
80g fresh parsley, finely
   chopped
1 onion, grated
½ tsp ground cinnamon
½ tsp freshly ground black
   pepper
1 tsp salt

Serving suggestion
Chickpeas with Tahini (page
   26)
Smoky Aubergine Dip (page
   38)
Yoghurt and Cucumber Salad
   (page 68) or a green salad

Preparation time: 20 minutes
Cooking time: 20 minutes

• Thoroughly mix all ingredients together as if you are kneading dough.

• Take some meat and roll into a ball. Push a skewer through it, spreading the meat tightly along it so it doesn't fall off it, making sure both ends are sealed tightly on the skewer.

• Grill or barbecue the meat for about 15 minutes until lightly browned on the outside. Serve hot.

Cook's tip
• I recommend using flat metal skewers to cook the meat on both sides because with flat skewers the meat doesn't turn when the skewers are turned over.

Okra Stew

Yakhnet Bameyeh

Okra, sometimes called ladies' fingers, is an acquired taste but very popular all over the Middle East. While cooking, minimise stirring to retain the shape of the okra and to prevent the development of a sticky texture. It's worth trying as the flavour is good.

SERVES 4

400g lamb or beef, cut into cubes
1 litre boiling water
3 tbsp oil
1 large onion, coarsely chopped
6 whole garlic cloves
$\frac{1}{2}$ tsp ground cinnamon
1 tsp salt
$\frac{1}{2}$ tsp ground pepper
1 tbsp tomato purèe
500g okra, top ends cut off
3 tomatoes, cut into quarters
Juice of 1 lemon or $\frac{1}{2}$ tbsp pomegranate molasses
30g chopped fresh coriander

Serving suggestion
Lebanese Rice with Vermicelli (page 228) or basmati rice

Preparation time: 20 minutes
Cooking time: 1–1 $\frac{1}{2}$ hours

• Put the meat in a large pan, pour over the water, then return to the boil. Cover and simmer gently for about 1 hour until the meat becomes tender. Drain, reserving the stock.

• Heat the oil and fry the onion for a few minutes until softened.

• Add the drained meat and fry for 3 minutes.

• Add the garlic, cinnamon, salt and pepper and stir for 1 minute.

• Add the meat stock, purèe, okra, tomatoes and lemon juice or molasses. Reserve a pinch of coriander to sprinkle over the top before serving, and stir the remainder into the pan.

• Simmer gently for about 30 minutes until the vegetables are cooked and the sauce is thickened.

Green Bean Stew

Yakhnet Loubeyeh

This is another everyday kind of food that all the family enjoy. It is an easy way to get young kids to eat green vegetables, and it is perfect for any variety of green beans.

SERVES 4

3 tbsp olive oil
250g onions, chopped
500g beef or lamb, diced
4 garlic cloves, crushed
$\frac{1}{2}$ tsp ground cinnamon
Freshly ground black pepper
100g tomato purèe
500ml boiling water
600g fresh green beans
1 tsp salt

Serving suggestion
Lebanese Rice with
   Vermicelli (page 228) or
   basmati rice

Preparation time: 15 minutes
Cooking time: 1–1$\frac{1}{2}$ hours

• Heat the oil and fry the onions for a few minutes until slightly brown.

• Add the meat cubes and fry with the onions until brown.

• Add the garlic, cinnamon and a twist of pepper and fry for 1–2 minutes.

• Dilute the tomato purèe in the boiling water, then add it to the meat, cover the pan, turn the heat down and allow to simmer for about 45 minutes until the meat is tender. Add a little more boiling water if needed.

• Trim the ends of the beans and cut them into smaller pieces, depending on the variety. Add to the meat with the salt and cook for another 20–30 minutes until the meat is well cooked, the beans are tender and everything is bathed in a rich, thick tomato sauce.

Stuffed Vegetables
Mehshi

Stuffed vegetables, mainly aubergines, courgettes and vine leaves, are traditional and popular in Lebanese cooking. Usually they are cooked together as a combination. Stuffed vegetables are a complete meal, having the vegetables, meat and rice in one dish.

SERVES 4

200g pudding rice
750g courgettes
400g baby aubergines
300g minced beef or lamb
2 tomatoes, grated
1½ tsp salt
½ tsp ground cinnamon
½ tsp freshly ground black
  pepper
50g tomato purèe
2 tsp dried mint
3 garlic cloves, crushed
Juice of 1 lemon

Preparation time: 1 hour
Cooking time: 1¼ hours

• Soak the rice while preparing the vegetables. Cut the tops off aubergines and courgettes and scoop out most of the inside.

• Rinse and drain the rice and mix with the meat, grated tomatoes, ½ tsp of the salt, cinnamon and pepper.

• Always when using a stuffing that includes rice, only ½ fill the vegetables, allowing for expansion and place in the pan.

• Mix the tomato purèe, mint, garlic, lemon and the remaining 1 tsp salt with water and add to the pan. The liquid should just cover the vegetables.

• Cover and allow to boil for 5 minutes, turn the heat down to medium and leave to simmer for about 1 hour until most of the sauce is absorbed.

• Some people put a layer of lamb chops in the base of the pan to create meatier and richer dish.

Baby Aubergines Filled with Mince
Sheikh el Mehshi

An impressive and tasty dish, this is one of many popular aubergine dishes which can be prepared in advance. I love serving this dish at dinner parties because it tastes good and looks good.

SERVES 4

12 small aubergines or 6
  large ones, sliced
1½ tsp salt
75ml oil
25g pine nuts (optional)
1 large onion, chopped
400g minced beef or lamb
1 tsp ground cinnamon
½ tsp pepper
2 tbsp tomato purèe
400ml hot water

Serving suggestion
Lebanese Rice with
  Vermicelli (page 228)

Preparation time: 1 hour
Cooking time: 1 hour

• Preheat the oven to 200°C/Gas 6.

• Part peel the aubergines so they look striped, sprinkle with 1 tsp of the salt and leave them aside for at least 1 hour. This stops the aubergines from absorbing too much oil while frying.

• Meanwhile, heat 50ml of the oil and fry the pine nuts, if using, for a few minutes to brown, then remove from the oil using a slotted spoon.

• Add the onion to the pan and fry for a few minutes until soft and beginning to brown.

• Add the mince and fry all together to brown, stirring to separate the grains.

• Add the cinnamon, the remaining salt and the pepper. Stir for another 2 minutes.

• Stir in the pine nuts and remove from the heat.

• Heat the remaining oil in a separate pan and fry the aubergines over a fairly high heat until brown.

• Slit each aubergine and fill with the mince. Arrange the aubergines in an oven-to-table dish with the filling facing upwards. Dilute the tomato purèe with the water and sprinkle with a little salt. Pour over the aubergines.

• Bake in the oven for 45 minutes until rich and thick.

Rolled Cabbage Leaves
Mehshi Malfoof

Stuffed vegetables are very popular in Lebanon and this version is economical and easy to prepare. It is a great combination of meat, vegetables and carbohydrate all in one, which looks complicated but is easy once you get the hang of it. You will need the thin variety of cabbage leaves such as January King. In some countries ordinary white cabbage leaves are thinner and easy to roll.

SERVES 4

1kg cabbage leaves
250g pudding rice or long-grain
400g coarse minced beef or lamb
2 tomatoes, chopped
1 tsp ground cinnamon
½ tsp freshly ground black pepper
1½ tsp salt
1 garlic bulb, divided into cloves, peeled and cut in halves or quarters if they are large
2 tbsp tomato purèe
2 tsp dried mint
Juice of 1 lemon

To garnish
1 tbsp chopped fresh mint

Preparation time: 40 minutes
Cooking time: 1 hour

• Separate the cabbage leaves and blanch in boiling water for few minutes to soften and make them easy to roll. Place leaves into a sieve to drain and cool.

• Rinse the rice, then drain off the water. Add the meat, tomatoes, cinnamon, pepper, 1 tsp of the salt and mix all these ingredients well.

• Remove and reserve the stalks in the middle of the cabbage leaves so each leaf is cut in half, or into quarters if they are too large. Place the leaves on a flat surface. Spoon about 3 tsp of the filling on each leaf and roll up firmly.

• Line the bottom of a large, heavy-based saucepan with the cabbage stalks. Cover with a layer of rolled cabbage and sprinkle with half the garlic. Add the remaining cabbage rolls and garlic.

• Mix the tomato purèe, mint and remaining salt, then dilute with about 300ml water. Pour over the cabbage, then add enough water so it just covers the top of the ingredients. Bring to the boil, then turn the heat down, cover and simmer gently for 1 hour.

• When most of the sauce has been absorbed, take out a cabbage roll and check that the rice is well cooked. If it is still undercooked, add a little more boiling water and cook for a little longer. When ready, add the lemon juice.

• Turn onto a flat serving dish. Sprinkle with little chopped mint and serve hot.

Butter Beans with Meat Stew
Yakhnet Fasoulia

This is a typical Lebanese stew that can be made with any type of beans or vegetables. You can use beef or lamb. Here I chose to use butter beans because I am passionate about them and so I hope you enjoy this recipe as much as I do.

SERVES 4

250g dried butter beans or
  600g cooked butter beans
40g butter or margarine
2 onions, chopped
500g beef or lamb, diced
5 garlic cloves, crushed
1 tsp ground cinnamon
1/2 tsp freshly ground black
  pepper
2 tbsp tomato purèe
1 litre water
1 tsp salt
60g chopped fresh coriander

Serving suggestion
Lebanese Rice with
  Vermicelli (page 228) or
  basmati rice

Preparation time: 15 minutes
Cooking time: 1 3/4 hours

• If you are using dried beans, soak them overnight in cold water. Drain, rinse, then place in a pan and cover with fresh water. Bring to the boil, then simmer for about 1 hour until you feel the beans are cooked (remember no salt before cooking or the beans will be tough). The time will vary depending on the variety and you may need to cook them for more than an hour. When ready, drain the beans.

• For a quicker meal, it is perfectly okay to use tinned beans, in which case, simply drain and rinse them.

• Melt the butter or margarine in a pan and fry the onions for a few minutes until they turn golden brown.

• Stir in the meat and fry until brown, stirring regularly.

• Add the garlic, cinnamon and pepper and stir for 3 minutes.

• Add the tomato purèe and water and bring to the boil. Cover the pan, turn the heat down and allow the stew to simmer for 1 hour until the meat has become tender.

• Add the beans and cook for a further 20 minutes.

• Finally, reserve a pinch of the coriander to garnish, then add the remainder to the pan with the salt. Cook for 5 minutes until the sauce is rich and thick. Beans absorb a lot of moisture even when they are already cooked, therefore if the sauce is too thick just add a little more boiling water until the sauce is the consistency you prefer.

Baked Kafta with Potatoes

Kafta Saneyeh

This dish is great for a quick and easy meal as it takes less than half an hour to prepare – plus children love it!

SERVES 4

500g minced beef or lamb
1 small onion, grated
50g fresh parsley, chopped
½ tsp ground cinnamon
Salt and freshly ground black
  pepper
1 large onion, thinly sliced
  into rings
500g potatoes, peeled and
  thinly sliced
4 tomatoes, sliced
2 tbsp tomato purèe
400ml water

To garnish
A few fresh parsley sprigs

Serving suggestion
Lebanese Rice with
  Vermicelli (page 228) or
  Pitta Bread (page 230)

Preparation time: 25 minutes
Cooking time: 1½ hours

- Preheat the oven to 220°C/Gas 7.

- Thoroughly mix the mince, grated onion, parsley, cinnamon, ½ tsp salt and a good twist of pepper.

- Wet the bottom of a 35–40cm baking dish with water and firmly spread the *kafta* over the base.

- Rub a little black pepper into the onion rings, then spread them over the *kafta*. Spread the potatoes over the onions, then spread the tomato slices over the top.

- Dilute the tomato purèe with the water and ½ tsp of salt, then pour over the top. Cover the dish with foil and cook in the oven for 30 minutes.

- Remove the foil and turn the oven down to 190°C/Gas 5 and cook for another 1 hour. Before removing from the oven, check the potatoes are well cooked and most of the sauce is absorbed and the surface is slightly crispy.

- Serve garnished with parsley.

Spinach with Minced Beef and Pine Nuts
Sabanekh ma Rouz

Even those in your family who don't much like spinach will enjoy eating spinach cooked this way. It's lemony and very quick and easy to cook. You can use frozen spinach, in which case, thaw the spinach and squeeze out all the water before using. Because there are no thickening ingredients in this recipe, it is important to reduce any unnecessary amount of fluid by boiling it off with the lid off the pan, otherwise it may look like soup.

SERVES 4

700g spinach, fresh or
    frozen, washed and
    chopped
50ml oil
15–20g pine nuts
2 onions, chopped
500g coarse minced beef
Juice of 1 large or 2 small
    lemons
1 heaped tsp ground
    cinnamon
$\frac{1}{2}$ tsp freshly ground black
    pepper
1 tsp salt
300ml boiling water

Serving suggestion
Lebanese Rice with
    Vermicelli (page 228)
Lemon wedges

Preparation time: 20 minutes
Cooking time: 1$\frac{1}{4}$ hours

• Rinse the spinach, then place in a colander to drain.

• Heat the oil in a large pan and fry the pine nuts for a few minutes to brown, then remove with a slotted spoon and put to one side.

• Add the onions to the oil and fry for about 10 minutes until golden brown.

• Add the meat and continue frying with the onions until the meat browns, stirring regularly.

• Add the cinnamon, pepper, salt and water and allow the mixture to boil for 5 minutes before you turn the heat down.

• Turn the heat down, cover the pan and simmer for 30 minutes.

• Stir in the spinach and lemon juice, cover and cook for another 40 minutes, making sure the sauce has reduced. If not, uncover the pan and continue to simmer for a few minutes to allow the excess moisture to evaporate.

• Stir half the pine nuts back into the pan and continue to cook for another couple of minutes so you get the most of the nutty flavour.

• Tip the mix into a serving dish and sprinkle with the remaining pine nuts.

Middle Eastern Pasta and Meat Bake
Macarouni

Middle Eastern people call any pasta *macarouni*. We don't have a wide range of pasta dishes, it's either cooked with mince and tomato sauce or with mince and white sauce. In this recipe I used penne.

SERVES 4

2 tbsp oil
2 onions, chopped
500g minced beef
1 tsp ground cinnamon
$\frac{1}{2}$ tsp salt
$\frac{1}{2}$ tsp freshly ground black
   pepper
350g penne
25g breadcrumbs

For the sauce
70g butter
80g plain flour
650ml milk
3 egg yolks, whisked
1 tsp salt

Serving suggestion
Tomato and Red Onion
   Salad (page 78) or a mixed
   green salad

Preparation time: 40 minutes
Cooking time: 1 hour

• Preheat the oven to 200°C/Gas 6.

• Heat the oil and fry the onions for a few minutes until lightly brown.

• Add the mince and fry with the onions, stirring, until brown.

• Add the cinnamon, salt and pepper and continue to stir for another minute. Remove from the heat.

• Now make the sauce. In a saucepan, melt the butter, stir in the flour and cook over a low heat for few minutes, stirring continuously, until all the butter is absorbed in the flour.

• Gradually whisk in a little milk at a time and keep stirring or whisking to avoid lumps.

• When all the milk is used up, keep stirring for another 2 minutes.

• Remove from the heat and stir in the whisked egg yolks.

• Meanwhile, cook the pasta in boiling salted water for about 8 minutes or as directed on the package, then turn onto a sieve to drain.

• Grease the bottom of a deep ovenproof dish (any shape will do) with a little butter, then spread half the pasta evenly over the dish. Pour over half the sauce to coat the pasta in the dish. Spread the meat mixture all over the first layer of pasta.

• Spread the remaining pasta over the meat and cover with the last of the sauce. Evenly sprinkle the breadcrumbs over the top.

• Bake in the oven for 45 minutes.

Beef Tortellini in Yoghurt
Shish Barak

This is a dish that takes longer to prepare but each step is not difficult. It's special and full of different flavours. The basis of this dish is homemade tortellini cooked in yoghurt and coriander. It's very unusual and I highly recommend you try it. The tortellini ingredients given here are just enough for this occasion. However, I usually make a much bigger batch of tortellini and freeze the surplus for future use. This makes this recipe a lot quicker to prepare.

SERVES 6

For the dough
250g plain flour, plus extra
   for rolling out
200ml cold water
½ tsp salt

For the filling
3 tbsp oil
1 onion, chopped
250g lean minced beef
½ tsp salt
½ tsp ground cinnamon
½ tsp freshly ground black
   pepper

For the yoghurt sauce
100g long-grain rice
1 tbsp cornflour
100ml cold water
2 litres plain yoghurt
1 tsp salt
4 garlic cloves, crushed
30g fresh coriander, chopped
30g butter

Preparation time: 1 hour
Cooking time: 1¼ hours

- Mix together all the dough ingredients and knead to a smooth and non-sticky dough. Wrap in clingfilm and chill in the fridge for half an hour.

- Heat the oil in a frying pan and fry the onion for a few minutes until lightly browned.

- Add the minced beef and fry to brown slightly, stirring regularly.

- When the mince and onions turn slightly brown, add the salt and spices, then stir for a further minute.

- Remove from the heat and leave aside to cool.

- On a floured work top, roll out the dough to about 3mm thick and cut into 6cm diameter circles with a round cutter or a small cup.

- Place 1 tsp of the filling on each circle, fold over into a semi-circle and seal all round the edge, then twist the two corners so they just overlap and stick them together.

- Cook the rice in boiling salted water until just tender, then drain.

- Blend the cornflour with the cold water until all the lumps disappear, then add to the yoghurt with the salt and stir together until the yoghurt looks very smooth.

- Bring the yoghurt mixture to the boil, stirring all the time to avoid separating, then add the cooked rice and continue to stir. After this stage, you don't have to stir other than occasionally.

- Now reduce the heat to low and leave to cook for about 30 minutes until the rice is almost dissolved, giving it the occasional gentle stir.

- When the sauce looks creamy, add the tortellini one by one so they don't stick together and cook for about 20 minutes.

- Finally, melt the butter in a frying pan, stir in the crushed garlic and fry for few seconds until it starts to change colour, then add all but 1 tbsp of the chopped coriander and stir for another few seconds. Finally add to the yoghurt, giving it a gentle quick stir, and cook for a further 5 minutes.

- Garnish with the reserved coriander and serve on its own.

Stuffed Artichoke Hearts
Ardi Shawki Mehshi

Artichokes are eaten all year round, mostly in salad or cooked whole and served with lemon dressing as a dip. This special dish is seldom cooked because of the hard work it involves. Peeling that amount of artichokes to get to the heart is seriously tedious. Like many people, I opt out by using frozen hearts or even tinned.

SERVES 4

50g cooking oil
25g pine nuts
250g onions, chopped
500g minced beef
20 artichoke hearts
½ tsp ground cinnamon
Salt and freshly ground black
   pepper
100g tomato purèe
700ml water

Serving suggestion
Lebanese Rice with
   Vermicelli (page 228)

Preparation time: 15 minutes
Cooking time: 1 hour

• Heat the oil and fry the pine nuts to brown, then remove from the oil with a slotted spoon and leave to one side.

• With the same oil, fry the onion for a few minutes. When it begins to brown, add the minced beef and fry together to brown.

• Add the fried pine nuts, cinnamon, salt and pepper and turn for one minute.

• Fill each artichoke heart with mince and place them neatly in a wide pan.

• Dilute the tomato purèe with the water and season with salt. Pour over the artichokes, cover the pan and cook on a low heat for 45 minutes until everything is tender.

Roast Beef with Garlic and Lemon
Rosto

When I invited friends for lunch and said that we were having roast beef, I could see the disappointment of their faces because they expected Lebanese food, not realising that we do roast beef in a very different way. And my friends have always enjoyed the experience of trying this version of roast beef. This may sound odd, but we usually serve rosto with Lebanese rice.

SERVES 6

2kg joint of beef
6 garlic cloves, cut vertically
   into 4 pieces
2 tbsp oil
1kg roasting potatoes
Juice of 2 lemons
500ml water
1 tsp of salt

Serving suggestion
Lebanese Rice with
   Vermicelli (page 228)

Preparation time: 20 minutes
Cooking time: $2\frac{3}{4}$ hours

• Preheat the oven to 190°C/Gas 5.

• With the point of a thin, sharp knife, make holes all round the joint and push a sliver of garlic into each hole.

• Heat the oil in a baking tin and brown the meat all round to seal and prevent the meat from drying.

• Roast the meat in the oven for 1 hour.

• Add the potatoes to the pan and return it to the oven to roast with the meat in the same baking tin for another hour until they have browned.

• Now mix the lemon juice with the water and salt, then pour it into the pan so the liquid is covering the potatoes. Return it to the oven for another 30–40 minutes, turning the joint few times, so it absorbs some of the sauce all round. If it looks too dry, just add little more water so you have a sauce.

• Slice the meat into chunky slices and place on a serving dish with the potatoes and pour the sauce over the top.

Potatoes with Mince and Eggs
Mfaraket Batata

This is an amazingly simple recipe, economical, tasty and quick to make. It takes 30 minutes to cook. You can serve it as a meal with salad or just as a quick snack.

SERVES 4

100ml cooking oil
800g potatoes, peeled and
  cubed
300g minced beef
4 eggs
½ tsp cinnamon
Salt and freshly ground black
  pepper

Serving suggestion
Pitta Bread (page 230)
Mixed green salad

Preparation time: 10 minutes
Cooking time: 30 minutes

• Heat the oil and fry the potatoes for about 10 minutes until golden brown.

• Add the mince and fry with potatoes until the mince looks brown and a bit crispy, stirring regularly.

• Crack the eggs into a bowl and whisk with a fork.

• Gradually pour into the potatoes and mince, stirring continuously to scramble the eggs.

• Finally sprinkle with cinnamon, salt and pepper and turn few times to blend in the spices.

Beef with Bulgur Wheat
Kebbeh Saneyeh

Kebbeh is a national dish of Lebanon. People used to spend many hours, first pounding the meat and then the whole mixture. In the mountains, some people still do. For most, the jorn (the huge pestle that contained the meat for pounding) is a thing of the past thanks to the invention of the electric food processor but the older generation still prefer to use the jorn energetically. My 80-year-old aunt still makes *kebbeh* in the old-fashioned way because she believes (like many others) that *kebbeh* made in the traditional way tastes better. *Kebbeh* is cooked in several different ways. When layered in a tray and baked in the oven, it is served as a main dish. *Kebbeh* Balls (page 48) can be cooked in yoghurt sauce and served with rice as a main dish or fried and served as starter.

SERVES 4

For the kebbeh
300g burghul (bulgur wheat)
300g minced beef
150g onion, grated
2 tsp fresh marjoram
1 tsp dried basil
1 tsp ground cumin
1 tsp salt
½ tsp freshly ground black
  pepper

For the filling
100ml oil
3 onions, chopped (about
  450g)
300g minced beef

• Rinse the burghul with cold water, drain immediately and leave for 30 minutes. The burghul then should be soft after absorbing the remaining moisture.

• Add all remaining *kebbeh* ingredients to the burghul and mix together with your hands, adding a little water at a time until it becomes like dough. Leave to rest while preparing the filling. Add little more water if it looks too stiff.

• In a frying pan, heat the oil and fry the onions for a few minutes until lightly brown.

• Add the meat and fry together with the onions to brown.

• Now add the walnuts or pine nuts, cinnamon, salt and pepper and stir together for a couple of minutes.

• Preheat the oven to 200°C/Gas 6 and grease a 35cm round baking tin, 6–7cm deep.

• Have a handy bowl of cold water near you while going through the following steps.

300g minced beef

45g chopped walnuts or 30g
  pine nuts (optional)

1 tsp ground cinnamon

1 tsp salt

1/2 tsp freshly ground black
  pepper

50ml olive oil

Serving suggestion
Salad with Lebanese Salad
  Dressing (page 233)
Yoghurt and Cucumber Salad
  (page 68) or plain yoghurt

Preparation time: 1 hour
Cooking time: 40–50
  minutes

- Divide the *kebbeh* into 2 portions and spread one portion to cover the bottom of the tin. Smooth the surface with wet hands.

- Spread the filling evenly all over the first layer of *kebbeh*.

- Take one handful of *kebbeh* at a time and flatten with your wet hands to no more than 2cm thick. Place it over the filling. Repeat the same method until you have covered all the filling. Wet your hands and smooth the surface well.

- Dip the end of a sharp knife in water, then cut the top layer of the *kebbeh* into small squares or diamond shapes (without cutting the bottom layer). Cut round the edge of the tin to detach the *kebbeh* from all round the edge.

- Drizzle a little olive oil over the top and bake for about 40–50 minutes until browned.

Courgettes Stuffed with Minced Beef and Pine Nuts

Ablama

I always remember this dish from childhood days. It was traditional to cook a feast at every wedding to feed the whole village. This is just one of the many special dishes they prepared that stuck in my head.

SERVES 4

6 tbsp oil
20g pine nuts
250g onions, chopped
300g minced beef
½ tsp ground cinnamon
1 tsp salt
½ tsp freshly ground black pepper
1kg small courgettes
2 tbsp tomato purèe
800ml water

Serving suggestion
Lebanese Rice with Vermicelli (page 228)

Preparation time: 1 hour
Cooking time: 30 minutes

• Heat half the oil and fry the pine nuts for a few minutes until brown, then remove from the pan with a slotted spoon and set aside.

• Add the onions to the pan and fry until they are lightly browned.

• Add the mince and fry, stirring, until browned.

• Season with cinnamon, ½ tsp of the salt and the pepper, then add the pine nuts and mix everything together.

• With a vegetable corer, scoop out the inside of the courgettes and fill them with the meat filling.

• Heat the remaining oil in a frying pan and shallow-fry the stuffed courgettes to brown all round, then place in a saucepan.

• Dilute the tomato purèe in the water and the remaining salt and pour over the courgettes. Cover and bring to the boil.

• Turn the heat down and cook for about 30 minutes until the sauce has thickened.

Potato and Beef Bake

Saneyeh Batata

This simple and extremely economical dish is so tasty and looks so appetising. It always goes down well with all the family including very young children

SERVES 4

1kg potatoes, peeled and
  sliced
50ml oil
2 onions, chopped
500g minced beef
1 tsp ground cinnamon
½ tsp freshly ground black
  pepper
100g tomato purèe
500ml hot water
1 tsp salt
Oil, for frying or roasting
  potatoes

Serving suggestion
Lebanese Rice with
  Vermicelli (page 228)

Preparation time: 30 minutes
Cooking time: 1 hour

• Preheat the oven to 200°C/Gas 6.

• Heat a little frying oil and fry the potato slices or, if you want to avoid frying, just roast in the oven to brown.

• Heat 50ml of oil and fry the onions until they become golden brown.

• Add the meat and fry together with the onions, stirring until browned.

• Add the cinnamon and pepper and stir for another minute.

• Arrange half the potatoes to cover the bottom of an ovenproof dish and spread the meat mixture over the top, then cover with the remaining potatoes.

• Dilute the tomato purèe with the hot water and salt, then pour over the top.

• Bake in the oven for about 40 minutes.

Beef and Potato Pie

Kebbeh Batata

This is what they call Poor Man's Kebbeh. The tasty filling of mince and onions turns this simple dish into a special, easy-to-serve meal.

SERVES 4

1kg potatoes, peeled and
  halved
100g butter
Salt and freshly ground black
  pepper
50ml oil
2 large onions, chopped
500g minced beef
1 tsp ground cinnamon
1 tbsp melted butter, for
  brushing
1 egg yolk
50g breadcrumbs

Serving suggestion
Mixed salad with Lebanese
  Salad Dressing (page 233)

Preparation time: 50 minutes
Cooking time: 1 hour

- Preheat the oven to 220°C/Gas 7 and grease a baking tin.

- Cook the potatoes in boiling water for about 10 minutes until soft, then drain well.

- Return them to the pan, add the butter and a little salt and mash the potatoes well.

- Heat the oil in a frying pan and fry the onions to brown slightly.

- Add the meat and fry together with the onions to brown.

- Add the cinnamon and a little salt and pepper and stir for another minute.

- Spread half the potatoes very smoothly to cover the base of the tin. Spread the meat filling evenly over the potatoes.

- Take a handful of the potatoes and flatten them between the palms of your hands, then place over the meat. Carry on until it is all covered with potatoes, then smooth the surface with wet palms.

- Brush the surface with melted butter, then with the egg yolk and sprinkle with breadcrumbs.

- Bake in the oven for 40 minutes until it's brown and crispy on the top.

- Allow this dish to cool a little so it can be easily sliced for serving.

Beef Cooked in Yoghurt

Laban Emmo

Looking at these few ingredients, it's hard to believe that they can create a great dish. It's low in fat but yet it tastes rich and tangy.

SERVES 4

500g beef, cubed
700ml water
40g oil or margarine
350g onions, halved and
   sliced
30g cornflour
2 tbsp water
1.4 litres plain yoghurt
Salt

Serving suggestion
Lebanese Rice with
   Vermicelli (page 228)

Preparation time: 20 minutes
Cooking time: 90 minutes

• Put the meat cubes in a pan with the water, bring to the boil, then simmer over a low heat for 45 minutes until the meat is almost tender and the liquid has reduced to a stock.

• Heat the oil or margarine and fry the onions for a few minutes until golden in colour.

• Drain the meat, reserving the stock.

• Add the meat to the onions and fry with onions until lightly browned, then return the meat and onions to the meat stock.

• Blend the cornflour with the water.

• Place the yoghurt in a saucepan and stir in the dissolved cornflour. Place over a low heat and stir continuously until it boils.

• Blend the yoghurt with the meat, stirring for few minutes, then cover and allow to simmer gently for 40 minutes. Season with salt.

• Then uncover the pan and simmer gently, allowing the yoghurt sauce to thicken and become creamy.

Stuffed Potatoes with Tomato Sauce
Mehshi Batata

Everybody loves stuffed potatoes. This dish always goes down well, even though it's a low-cost recipe. You'll never be embarrassed to serve it, even at a dinner party.

SERVES 4

Oil, for frying
200g onions, chopped
250g minced beef
½ tsp ground cinnamon
Salt and freshly ground black
  pepper
12 potatoes
60g tomato purée
500ml water

Serving suggestion
Plain rice

Preparation time: 1 hour
Cooking time: 45 minutes

- Preheat the oven to 200°C/Gas 6.

- Heat 3 tbsp of oil and fry the onions for a few minutes until they start to brown.

- Add the mince and keep frying together to brown.

- Add the cinnamon, ½ tsp salt and a twist of pepper and stir for 1–2 minutes.

- Peel the potatoes and hollow out some of the middles.

- Heat a little oil and fry or roast the potatoes for 15–20 minutes to brown, then allow to cool slightly.

- Fill the potatoes with the meat filling and place in an ovenproof dish. Dilute the tomato purèe in the water with 1 tsp salt, then pour over the potatoes.

- Bake in the oven for 40 minutes.

Pea, Carrot and Beef Stew

Yakhnet Bazella

Stews are an every day family dish that everyone enjoys, particularly children. When my children were very young and had their friends for dinner after school, they always requested bazella; for some reason it always appealed to very young children. There is a huge variety of stews with different vegetables or pulses but this is one you will cook frequently.

SERVES 4

30ml olive oil
500g beef, diced
1 large onion, chopped
4 garlic cloves, crushed
1/2 tsp ground cinnamon
1 tsp salt
1/2 tsp freshly ground black
    pepper
1 litre boiling water
2 tbsp tomato purèe
2–3 carrots, peeled and
    sliced
500g frozen peas
20g chopped fresh coriander
Juice of 1 lemon (optional)

Serving suggestion
Lebanese Rice with
    Vermicelli (page 228)

Preparation time: 20 minutes
Cooking time: 1 1/2 hours

- Heat the oil and fry the onion until slightly brown.

- Add the meat and stir over a medium-high heat until it starts to brown.

- Add the garlic and stir for another minute.

- Now add the cinnamon, salt and pepper and stir for a further minute.

- Add the water and tomato purèe, cover the pan and simmer for about 1 hour until the sauce has thickened.

- Add the carrots and cook for 10 minutes.

- Add the peas and cook for 20 minutes.

- Reserve a little of the coriander, then stir in the remainder and cook for 5 minutes.

- Add the lemon juice, if liked, and serve sprinkled with the reserved coriander.

Lemon Chicken

Djaj be Hamoud

This amazingly easy-to-prepare dish, with only a few flavourful ingredients, will surprise you with its strong flavours. You can cut up a whole chicken or just use chicken breasts.

SERVES 4

1 medium-size chicken, cut
  the chicken into 8 pieces
  with the skin on
800g potatoes, peeled and
  cut into cubes
4 tbsp olive oil
80g fresh coriander, chopped
4 garlic cloves, chopped
100ml lemon juice
1 tsp salt
1/2 tsp freshly ground black
  pepper

Serving suggestion
Roasted mixed vegetables

Preparation time: 10 minutes
Cooking time: 1 1/4 hours

• Preheat the oven to 200°C/Gas 6.

• Place the chicken and potatoes in a baking tin and drizzle with half the oil. Roast in the oven for 1 hour until they turn brown.

• Mix the coriander, garlic, lemon juice, remaining oil, salt and pepper and spread this sauce all over the chicken and potatoes.

• Cover with kitchen foil and return to the oven for another 15 minutes until cooked through.

• Remove from the oven and transfer to a serving dish.

Chicken with Aubergines and Rice
Makloubeh

This is a Palestinian national dish and with the presence of many Palestinians in Lebanon in the last fifty years, *makloubeh* has become a popular home-cooked dish.

SERVES 4

600g aubergines, cut into 4cm thick slices
3 tsp salt
250g long-grain rice
Oil, for frying
400g onions, halved and sliced
500g chicken breasts, cut into cubes
1 tsp ground cinnamon
$\frac{1}{2}$ tsp grated nutmeg
$\frac{1}{2}$ tsp freshly ground black pepper
500ml boiling water

To garnish
Sprinkling of chopped fresh parsley
1 small tomato, chopped
Pine nuts (optional)

Serving suggestion
Mixed salad
Plain yoghurt

Preparation time: 15 minutes plus soaking
Cooking time: 1$\frac{1}{4}$ hours

- Sprinkle 2 tsp of salt over the aubergines and leave in a sieve to draw out the moisture from the aubergine; most of the salt will wash out with it. Leave for a couple of hours, then lightly squeeze the slices.

- Meanwhile, soak the rice in water for 1 hour.

- Heat a little oil, and fry the aubergine slices for about 20 minutes to brown on both sides. Alternatively, if you want to avoid frying, just drizzle a little oil on the aubergines and roast in a hot oven to brown.

- Heat a little oil in a large pan and fry the onions until they turn golden.

- Add the chicken and fry to brown.

- Add the cinnamon, nutmeg and, remaining 1 tsp salt and the pepper and stir well.

- Add the boiling water, cover the pan and simmer gently for 20 minutes.

- Add the aubergines to the chicken and onions.

- Drain the rice and spread over the top.

- Making sure the water is level with the rice, return to the boil, cover and simmer gently for about 20 minutes until all the water is absorbed and the rice is cooked. If the rice is undercooked just add a little water and cook for a few more minutes.

- Turn off the cooker and allow the rice to settle for 2 minutes.

- Remove the lid, cover the pan with a flat serving dish and carefully turn it upside down so the pan is resting on the dish, then gently remove the pan so everything remains in layers.

- Garnish with parsley, tomato and pine nuts to serve.

Chicken with Rice and Nuts
Djaj ma Rouz

This dish is always served at special occasions or any large gathering. It is very simple to prepare and the nuts on the top make it look grand and appetising. Also it is a great dish for the family, as it is simple enough to cook any day.

SERVES 4

1 medium to large whole
  chicken
4 x 5cm cinnamon sticks
$\frac{1}{2}$ tsp freshly ground black
  pepper
1 tsp salt
$\frac{1}{2}$ tsp mixed spice
500g long-grain rice
50ml oil
100g split or flaked almonds
30g pine nuts
100g minced beef
1 tsp ground cinnamon

Serving suggestion
Mixed salad
Plain yoghurt

Cooking time: 90 minutes

• Cut the chicken into quarters and place in a pan with the cinnamon sticks, pepper, salt and mixed spice. Just cover with boiling water.

• Return to the boil, then allow to simmer for 1 hour until the chicken is tender.

• Uncover the pan and boil to reduce the stock to about one-third.

• Meanwhile, soak the rice in cold water.

• In a frying pan, heat the oil and fry the almonds for a few minutes to brown, then remove from the oil.

• Add the pine nuts to the same oil and fry until brown, then remove from the oil and mix with the almonds.

• Next add the minced beef to the pan and fry until crispy and brown, stirring regularly.

• Add the ground cinnamon and fry for a few seconds, stirring well.

• Drain the rice and add it to the mince with a little more salt to taste.

• Add the stock to the rice and mince to cover it by 1cm. Bring to the boil, then reduce the heat to low, cover the pan and cook for about 20 minutes until all the stock is absorbed.

• Turn the rice mixture onto a flat serving dish. Bone the chicken and place on top of the rice and sprinkle all the nuts over the top.

Marinated Chicken Kebabs
Djaj Tawouk

Mixed grill is usually barbecued *tawouk*, *kafta* and lamb cubes, but you can choose to do one of the three. *Tawouk* is one of the simplest and most tasty ways to eat chicken. The marinated chicken can be barbecued or grilled.

SERVES 4

4 skinless chicken breasts,
   cut into chunky cubes
1 red pepper, cut into chunks
1 yellow pepper, cut into
   chunks

For the marinade
4 garlic cloves, crushed
1 tbsp mayonnaise
3 tbsp plain yoghurt
2 tbsp olive oil
2 tbsp lemon juice
½ tsp chilli powder
   (optional)
1 tsp paprika
½ tsp salt

Serving suggestion
Pitta Bread (page 230)
Dips
Mixed salad

Preparation time: 15 minutes
   plus marinating
Cooking time: 20 minutes

• Place the chicken in a non-metallic bowl.

• Mix together all the marinade ingredients. Place the chicken in the marinade, cover and leave in the fridge for at least 6 hours or overnight.

• Thread the chicken on to skewers alternately with chunks of pepper.

• Cook for 20 minutes on a preheated grill or barbecue, making sure the centre is well cooked and the outside slightly caramelised so the chicken is moist. Don't overcook or the chicken will quickly become dry.

Garlic Chicken

Djaj ma Toum

When I serve this dish to people who are not familiar with using this quantity of garlic in one dish, I look for the shock on their faces and watch as the garlic is pushed to one side of the plate. Be bold – give it a try! When you've tried one clove, you'll realise how mild the garlic becomes when cooked. After that, you wouldn't have one mouthful of chicken without the garlic

SERVES 4

4 tbsp olive oil
1 large free-range chicken, quartered
3 whole bulbs of garlic, cloves separated and peeled
1/2 tsp salt

Serving suggestion
Green Beans with Tomatoes (page 166)

Preparation time: 20 minutes
Cooking time: 1 hour

- Preheat the oven to 190°C/Gas 5.

- Heat the olive oil and fry the chicken pieces over a high heat to brown and seal the skin. Place the chicken pieces in a casserole dish, together with oil from frying.

- Sprinkle the garlic over the chicken, cover the dish and cook in the oven for 1 hour until cooked through and tender.

- Season with salt and return to the oven for 5 minutes before serving.

Arabian Cardamom Chicken

Kabseh

Over the years, *kabseh* has become one of the regular dishes in Lebanon. It has been imported to Lebanon by the Lebanese living in Saudi Arabia and the large number of Saudi tourists who come to Lebanon. Don't let the long list of ingredients put you off because they are mostly basic ingredients that you'll already have in your kitchen.

SERVES 4

1 medium chicken
½ large onion, quartered
4 garlic cloves
2 x 10cm cinnamon sticks
1 tsp black peppercorns
10 cardamom pods
Salt
1 litre boiling water

For the rice
50ml oil
100g onion, finely chopped
125g carrots, finely diced
1 green pepper, chopped
1 garlic clove, crushed
1 tsp salt
½ tsp ground cardamom
½ tsp freshly ground black
   pepper
1 tsp ground cumin
400g basmati rice

For the sauce
30ml oil
50g onions, chopped
2 garlic cloves
1 hot chilli, chopped
   (optional)
½ tsp salt
500g chopped fresh
   tomatoes

• Soak the rice in cold water for 1 hour.

• Cut the chicken into halves or quarters and place in a large saucepan with the onions, garlic, cinnamon sticks, peppercorns, cardamom pods and salt. Add the boiling water and allow the chicken to boil on a high heat for 10 minutes.

• Cover the pan, turn the heat to medium and allow the chicken to cook for about 45 minutes until it feels tender and well cooked.

• While the chicken is cooking, prepare the sauce. Heat the oil and fry the onions until they become golden brown.

• Add the garlic, chilli and salt and stir for another minute or so.

• Add the chopped tomatoes, cover and simmer gently on a low heat so it cooks in its own juices without having to add any water. Cook for 15 minutes. If it looks too thick, add a little water.

• Remove the chicken from the stock and leave aside to cool a little while you prepare the sauce and the rice. Drain and reserve the stock.

• To make the rice, heat the oil and fry the almonds until brown, then remove from the oil.

• With the same oil, start by frying the onions to soften, then add the carrots, peppers and garlic and stir-fry for 5 minutes.

• Add the salt, ground cardamom, pepper and ground cumin and stir for another 2 minutes until all the vegetables have softened.

• Drain the rice, then mix with the vegetables. Pour in enough of the reserved stock to cover the rice by 1cm. Bring to the boil, then boil for about 3 minutes until most of the water has evaporated.

Serving suggestion
Yoghurt and Cucumber Salad
(page 68) or plain yoghurt

Preparation time: 15 minutes
plus soaking
Cooking time: 1¾ hours

• Cover the pan, turn the heat to low and cook very gently for about 20 minutes to allow all the moisture to evaporate so the rice looks dry and the grains separate.

• Bone the chicken. Turn the rice onto a round, flat serving dish, place the chicken pieces on top and sprinkle with the almonds.

• Heat the tomato sauce and serve with the chicken and rice.

Fish with Mixed Peppers

Samak bil Fleifleh

This colourful dish is quick to prepare. It can be served as main course or as a cold starter with bread on the side.

SERVES 4

500g skinless fillets of any
  white fish of your choice
2 tbsp olive oil
1 large onion, diced
4 garlic cloves, crushed
1 green chilli pepper, thinly
  sliced (optional)
1 red chilli pepper, thinly
  sliced (optional)
300g red, green and yellow
  peppers, diced
60g fresh coriander, chopped
Salt and freshly ground black
  pepper

Serving suggestion
Lemony Potato Salad (page
  70)

Preparation time: 15 minutes
Cooking time: 30 minutes

- Preheat the oven to 200°C/Gas 6.

- Bake the fish in the oven for 15 minutes.

- Meanwhile, heat the oil and fry the onion for a few minutes to soften.

- Add the garlic and chilli, if using, and stir for a couple of minutes.

- Now add the diced peppers and stir-fry for 3 minutes. Cover and allow all the mixture to soften.

- Add the coriander and salt and cook for a few more minutes.

- Bring the fish out of the oven and spread the pepper mix over the top, then return to the oven for 10 minutes.

Baked Fish in Tahini Sauce

Samakeh Harrah

This is a speciality fish dish in Tripoli, north of Lebanon. When you visit this old city, you head to the seafront for *samakeh harrah*, which means hot fish. After that you head to the sweet shop for dessert to have another speciality *halawet el jibin*, if you manage to save space for it. My husband highly recommends peas with this dish. Even though it's not a Lebanese way, I agree with him.

SERVES 4

2 tbsp oil
20g pine nuts (optional)
200g onions, halved and
   thinly sliced
1kg white fish fillets, such as
   cod or haddock
100ml tahini
50ml lemon juice
160ml cold water
$\frac{1}{2}$–1 tsp chilli powder
1 tsp salt
Chopped fresh parsley

To garnish
Pine nuts

Serving suggestion
Cumin Rice (page 154 or
   Pitta Bread (page 230)
Roasted Cauliflower (page
   168, without the tahini
   sauce)

Preparation time: 20 minutes
Cooking time: 50 minutes

• Preheat the oven to 200°C/Gas 6.

• Heat the oil in a frying pan and fry the pine nuts until browned, then remove from the pan and leave aside.

• Add the onions to the same oil and fry until soft and very slightly brown.

• Place the fish in an ovenproof dish and spread the onions over it.

• In a bowl, mix the tahini with the lemon juice so it becomes dry and fluffy.

• Add the cold water a little at a time, stirring continuously, until it gets to single cream thickness. Add the chilli powder and salt and pour over the fish and onions.

• Bake in the oven for 30 minutes until very slightly brown on top.

• Sprinkle with pine nuts to serve.

Rice with Cumin

Rouz ma Cammoon

Baked Fish in Tahini Sauce (page 152) is usually served with Lebanese bread, but my own preference is to serve it with this cumin rice as it complements the flavours perfectly and balances the richness of the tahini.

SERVES 4

300g basmati rice
2 tbsp olive oil
50g onion, chopped
1 tsp ground cumin
½ tsp salt
Freshly ground black pepper
2 tbsp browned pine nuts
   (optional)

Preparation time: 5 minutes
   plus soaking
Cooking time: 30 minutes

- Soak the rice in cold water for 1 hour.

- Heat the oil and fry the onion to become slightly brown

- Add the cumin, salt and pepper and stir for another minute.

- Drain the rice, then add it to the pan and just cover with boiling water. Allow to boil for about 3 minutes until most of the water has evaporated.

- Turn the heat to low, cover and allow to cook for 15 minutes until all the moisture has evaporated. Serve sprinkled with pine nuts, if liked.

Fish with Saffron Rice

Sayadiyeh

Fish is often eaten but usually in a very simple presentation, either fried or baked and always served with tahini sauce. However, this special dish, *sayadiyeh*, will become one of your favourites. A friend of mine never liked fish until she turned up one day and I had just made *sayadiyeh* for dinner. She joined us (being polite) and after that she became a fan of fish dishes.

SERVES 4

A few threads of saffron
50ml hot water
300g basmati rice
4 tbsp olive oil
40g split almonds
20g pine nuts
700g fillets of light white fish
Flour, for coating fish
400g onions, halved and
   thinly sliced
1 tsp ground cumin
Salt and freshly ground black
   pepper
Sprinkling of chopped fresh
   parsley

Serving suggestion
Tahini Salad (page 71)

Preparation time: 10 minutes
Cooking time: 1 hour

• Soak the saffron in the hot water. I do this a few hours before cooking so it's ready to use at any time and the water has turned yellow. By doing this, you get more colour and flavour in the rice.

• Rinse the rice thoroughly and allow to soak in water for 30 minutes to 1 hour.

• Heat 2 tbsp of the oil and fry the almonds until browned, then remove from the pan and fry the pine nuts until golden brown, then remove from the pan.

• Heat the remaining oil in a large frying pan. Coat the fish with flour on both sides and shallow-fry for about 5–10 minutes each side until browned, turning once. Remove from the pan.

• Add the onions to the fish-flavoured oil and fry them until they turn golden brown.

• Drain the rice.

• Add the cumin and salt and pepper to taste to the onions and stir for 1–2 minutes.

• With the onions in the bottom of the pan, place the fish over the onions and add the drained rice.

• Cover with water to 1cm above the rice level and allow it to boil for about 3 minutes until the water has gone down to the rice level.

• Now add the saffron juice to the rice and stir gently to form a few yellow ripples. Turn the heat to low, cover the pan and simmer for 20 minutes until there is no excess water left.

• Uncover the pan and remove from the heat. Place a serving plate on the pan facing down and turn the pan upside-down and slowly remove the pan.

• Sprinkle all the nuts over the top and garnish with little chopped parsley.

Chilli Fish with Fresh Coriander
Beiruti Samakeh Harrah

This is *samakeh harrah* the Beirut way. It can be served warm but usually it's served cold with bread. It is very simple and an extremely tasty dish. It is a great dish for chilli lovers but you can cook it without chilli and it's still full of flavour.

SERVES 4

2$\frac{1}{2}$kg whole white fish or
  1kg light fish fillets
100ml olive oil
5 garlic cloves, finely
  chopped
2 green chillies, seeded and
  chopped, or more if you
  prefer it very hot
200g fresh coriander,
  chopped
$\frac{1}{4}$ tsp cayenne pepper
$\frac{1}{2}$ tsp salt
Freshly ground black pepper

Serving suggestion
Potato Special with Peppers
  (page 172)

Preparation time: 30 minutes
Cooking time: 35 minutes

- Preheat the oven to 200°C/Gas 6.

- If you are cooking whole fish, wrap it in foil and bake in the oven for 20 minutes. Allow to cool.

- Heat the oil in a frying pan over a medium heat and stir in the garlic and chilli, if using. Fry for few seconds without allowing the garlic to brown.

- Add the coriander and stir-fry with the garlic and chilli for a couple of minutes. Season with salt, cayenne and black pepper to taste.

- Open the fish down the middle to remove all the bones and skin, then spread some of the coriander mixture between the two sides.

- Reconstruct the fish and cover with the remaining coriander.

- Cover the fish and leave to cool completely so that all the flavours are absorbed.

Lebanese Omelette

Egget Baiyd Lebnaneyeh

This substantial omelette is tasty, quick and simple plus the fact that it's quite filling enough to serve as a quick meal any time.

SERVES 4

6 large eggs
½ tsp cinnamon
Salt to taste
Freshly ground black pepper
90g onions, chopped
40g fresh parsley, chopped
2 tbsp olive oil

Serving suggestion
Mixed green salad and
   tomato salad
Lemony Potato Salad (page
   70) or Potato and Pepper
   Special (page 172)

Preparation time: 5–10
   minutes
Cooking time: 10 minutes

• Whisk the eggs with the cinnamon, salt and pepper.

• Add the onions and parsley and mix well.

• Heat the oil in a frying pan, around 25cm in diameter.

• Turn the heat down to medium and pour in the egg mixture. Allow about 5 minutes for the bottom of the omelette to brown.

• Now either turn the omelette to brown the top or simply place it under the grill until it becomes golden brown.

CHAPTER 5
Vegetable and Pulse Main Dishes
Aklaat Nabatiyeh

In this vegetarian section you will experience and enjoy the tasty meals that the Lebanese enjoy eating. You don't come across many vegetarians in Lebanon, but they all enjoy the traditional variety of recipes for vegetables and pulses. I am not a vegetarian but I often cook vegetarian meals because they are part of our diet and always enjoyed by everyone.

When I have dinner parties, naturally I make a selection of dishes and it is always important to include vegetarian dishes which are enjoyed by my guests. In Lebanon, people tend to express their generosity by providing meat dishes, but still never without a variety of vegetarian options, which always bring back the traditional taste of peasant food.

Fried Aubergines with Tomatoes
Maghmoura

This is one of my favourite cold dishes. It is always served cold with bread, either as a starter or as a side dish. Because of the fantastic flavour of this simple dish I love eating it as a snack with bread and nothing else. You may peel the skin of the aubergines or leave it on. I like to keep the skin on for holding the shape of the slices and also because it contains vitamins.

SERVES 4

2 aubergines, cut into 2cm thick slices
Salt
Oil, for frying aubergines
1 tbsp olive oil
3 garlic cloves, chopped
3 chillies, chopped (optional)
4 tomatoes, halved and sliced

To serve
2 tbsp chopped fresh parsley or mint leaves (optional)

Serving suggestion
Pitta Bread (page 230)

Preparation time: 20 minutes plus standing
Cooking time: 45 minutes

• Sprinkle the aubergine slices generously with salt and leave in a sieve for a minimum of 1 hour, allowing the salt to draw out the water from the aubergines. This treatment ensures that the aubergines don't absorb too much oil while frying and is vital to giving the right final texture.

• Heat a little oil in a frying pan. Gently squeeze aubergines to extract any moisture you can, then fry the aubergine slices to brown on both sides. When brown, place on kitchen paper to absorb any excess oil.

• Remove the frying oil from the pan and heat the olive oil. Stir in the garlic and chillies, if using, and fry for few seconds, making sure you don't allow the garlic to brown.

• Add the tomatoes. Stir all the ingredients together. Season with salt and allow to simmer on a gentle heat for 3–4 minutes.

• Put the aubergine slices on a serving dish and spread tomato mixture over the top. Allow to cool. Sprinkle a little parsley or mint leaves on top and serve cold with pitta bread.

Green Beans with Tomatoes
Loubeyeh Bzeit

This is a lovely way to serve any kind of green beans, fresh or frozen. You'll never make too much of it because it is usually served cold as a side dish and makes perfect snacks. This dish should cook in its own juices so avoid adding water unless it looks dry. It can be eaten hot but most people, including me, prefer to eat it cold.

SERVES 4

500g stringless, runner or
   french beans
4 tbsp olive oil
1 large onion, chopped
1 whole bulb of garlic,
   separated into cloves and
   peeled
500g fresh tomatoes,
   chopped, or canned
   tomatoes
1 tsp salt

Preparation time: 20 minutes
Cooking time: 50 minutes

* Trim the beans and roughly cut into 5cm pieces.

* Heat 3 tbsp of the oil and fry the onions and garlic cloves to brown slightly.

* Add the beans and mix with the onions and garlic. Reduce the heat, cover and simmer for about 5 minutes until the beans are tender, turning occasionally.

* Add the tomatoes and salt and cook gently for 30 minutes until the tomatoes have turned into a lovely thick sauce.

* Turn off the heat and stir in the remaining tbsp of olive oil. Leave to cool before serving.

Roasted Cauliflower with Tahini Sauce
Karnabeet Ma Tahini

This is my favourite way of eating cauliflower and everyone who tried it agreed with me. It can be served as a starter with bread or as a side dish, and the cauliflower can be fried or baked to brown. Burnt cauliflower is what Sami, my six-year-old grandson calls it. It's one of his favourite foods.

SERVES 4

1 large cauliflower, broken
   into florets
½ tsp salt
2 tbsp olive oil

For the tahini sauce
50ml lemon juice
1 garlic clove, crushed
Salt
100ml tahini
120ml cold water

Preparation time: 15 minutes
Cooking time: 40–50
   minutes

* Heat the oven to 200°C/Gas 6.

* Rinse the cauliflower and place in a baking tray. Sprinkle with salt and drizzle with oil and turn well to coat all the florets with oil and salt.

* Bake for about 40 minutes, making sure the cauliflower is well browned.

* To make the dip, add the lemon juice, salt and garlic to the tahini and mix well. When it goes all thick and fluffy, start adding a little water at a time while blending into the mixture until it becomes like cream for dipping.

Cook's tip
* Also, you may add chopped parsley and chopped tomatoes to turn this into a tahini salad.

Stuffed Vine Leaves

Warak Inab

Stuffed vine leaves are very popular in Lebanon and always served at dinner parties as part of the spread and buffets. They are always served cold, which makes it a great dish to prepare in advance, even better the day before. They look hard to do but, in fact, they are quite easy, and once you've done the first five or ten it gets easier and quicker. The vine leaves must be young and tender so if fresh ones are not available, they are often bought tinned in brine.

SERVES 4

400–500g fresh vine leaves
1 potato, peeled and sliced
140g fresh flatleaf parsley, chopped
30g fresh mint, chopped
450g tomatoes, chopped
1 bunch or 100g spring onions, chopped
250g pudding rice
2 tbsp lemon juice
4 tbsp olive oil
1 tsp salt

Preparation time: 1½ hours
Cooking time: 1 hour

• Prepare the fresh leaves by dipping in boiling water for 1 minute to soften and make rolling possible. If you are using vine leaves in brine, just rinse with fresh water to rinse off the salt, then drain.

• Line the base of a saucepan with potato slices to prevent the rolled leaves from sticking to the pan; also I like them as they absorb the lemony sauce.

• To make the filling, mix all the remaining ingredients except 2 tbsp of the oil, allowing 15 minutes for it to soften and the rice swell a little by absorbing some of the lemon and oil.

• Place the shiny side of the leaves face down and place about 1–2 tsp of the filling on the matt side of each leaf. Fold the sides over the filling, then fold over the end which is towards you and roll firmly towards the end of the leaf and place them in the pot on top of the potatoes.

• Add enough water almost to cover the leaves but make sure they are exposed at the top so they don't float and come undone.

• Bring to the boil and boil for a few minutes, then turn the heat down, add the remaining 2 tbsp olive oil, which makes the leaves look shiny, cover the pan and simmer for about 1 hour until the water has evaporated.

• Test one roll to make sure the rice is well cooked; if not, add a little more water and cook a little longer.

• Allow to cool, then turn onto a serving dish.

Potato Special with Peppers
Batata be Fleifleh

I was having dinner at my friend's restaurant and among the many dishes served was this potato dish that was a speciality. I really enjoyed it, then tried to memorise the ingredients to make it at home. When I saw my friend I told him that I was including their recipe in the book; then he told me that they didn't make it with peppers, but he liked the idea. So I emailed him the recipe and now it's on their menu.

SERVES 4

100ml olive oil
800g potatoes, peeled and
   cut into small cubes
250g onions, halved and
   sliced
6 whole garlic cloves
250g red, green and yellow
   peppers, cut into chunks
1 tsp salt
Juice of ½ a lemon

To garnish
Lemon wedges

Preparation time: 20 minutes
Cooking time: 30 minutes

• Heat the oil and fry the potatoes until they brown slightly, then cover for a few minutes until cooked.

• Add the onions and garlic cloves and fry for a few minutes until the onions look soft, then add the peppers and fry them all together. Cover the pan for few more minutes until everything is cooked.

• Stir in the salt and lemon juice.

• Garnish with lemon wedges and serve at once with any meat, chicken or fish.

Okra With Tomatoes, Garlic and Coriander
Bameyeh Bzeit

This is a vegetarian okra dish. It can be served as main dish with rice or served cold with bread.

SERVES 4

4 tbsp olive oil
300g onions, chopped into
   large pieces
8 garlic cloves
500g fresh okra, tops
   trimmed
450g tomatoes, diced
1 tsp salt
100g fresh coriander,
   chopped
1 tbsp pomegranate molasses
   or juice of $\frac{1}{2}$ lemon

Preparation time: 20 minutes
Cooking time: 40 minutes

• Heat 3 tbsp of the olive oil in a pan and fry the onions and garlic until they begin to brown.

• Add the okra, stir well, cover and simmer for 15 minutes, turning occasionally.

• Add the tomatoes and salt. Reserve a little coriander to sprinkle on the top, and add the remainder to the pan. Simmer for a further 20 minutes, allowing most of the juice to evaporate.

• Finally add the remaining 1 tbsp olive oil with the pomegranate molasses or lemon juice and sprinkle the reserved coriander over the top.

Aubergines with Chickpeas
Mnazaleh

This nutritious vegetarian peasant dish is usually served cold with bread as a main or side dish. It is one of the dishes that was served on days when the meat at the local butcher in the village was sold out.

SERVES 4

5 tbsp olive oil
280g onions, chopped
6 garlic cloves
2 aubergines, cubed, about
  600g
300g tomatoes, chopped
1 tbsp tomato purèe
1 tsp salt
250ml water
400g cooked chickpeas

Preparation time: 15 minutes
Cooking time: 1 hour

• Heat 4 tbsp of the oil and fry the onions and garlic until slightly brown.

• Add the aubergines and fry for few minutes.

• Add the tomatoes, tomato purèe, salt and water and cook for 15 minutes.

• Add the chickpeas and cook for a further 15 minutes, allowing most of the moisture to evaporate.

• When cooking is complete, stir in the remaining olive oil for extra flavour, then turn onto a serving dish and leave to cool.

Fried Aubergines with Potato Filling
Batingan ma Batata

Fried aubergines are always served with fried potatoes, courgettes, onions and tomatoes. When someone says they are having a mixed fry-up, that always means fried vegetables. A little while ago I decided to have a bit of fun by combining aubergines and potatoes into one dish and this was my result. Serve it with any meat dish, with salad, or just by itself.

SERVES 4

2 aubergines, about 700g, cut into 1cm thick slices
Salt
Oil, for frying
300g onions, halved and thinly sliced
3 garlic cloves, sliced
800g potatoes, peeled and diced

Preparation time: 30 minutes plus standing
Cooking time: 1 hour

- Sprinkle the aubergines with salt, then leave in a colander for at least 1 hour. This stops the aubergines from absorbing too much oil when frying.

- Heat 3 tbsp oil and fry the onions to brown slightly.

- Add the garlic and potatoes and stir-fry them all together.

- Add a pinch of salt, turn down the heat, cover the pan and allow the potatoes to cook gently, turning occasionally, for about 15 minutes until well cooked.

- Heat a frying pan with enough oil to shallow-fry the aubergines. Before frying, squeeze as much water as you can from the aubergines or place them on kitchen paper to absorb the water. Fry the slices to brown on both sides.

- Preheat the oven to 200°C/Gas 6.

- Line the side and base of a round oven dish with about two-thirds of the aubergines and spoon the potatoes into the dish. Cover with remaining aubergine slices and bake in the oven for 10 minutes.

- When you take the dish out of the oven, place a flat serving plate over the top and turn it upside down. Remove the oven dish and serve.

Green Lentils with Rice and Caramelised Onions
Mdardara

Mdardara is another low-cost dish that is popular across Lebanon. With only a few ingredients, the caramelised onions give it this unique flavour. It is always served with a salad or just plain yoghurt. Remember not to salt pulses while they are cooking as they will toughen.

SERVES 4

250g long-grain rice
250g green lentils
1 litre water
100ml olive oil
3 onions, sliced
1 tsp salt

Serving suggestion
Mixed green salad
Plain yoghurt

Preparation time: 20 minutes
   plus soaking
Cooking time: 1¼ hours

• Soak the rice in cold water for 30 minutes.

• Meanwhile, cook lentils in the water for 40 minutes until just cooked.

• Drain the lentils, keeping the stock aside for cooking the rice.

• Heat the oil and fry the onions for about 20 minutes until caramelised and crispy.

• With a slotted spoon, remove the onions from the oil. Keep the oil to add to the rice.

• Drain the rice and place it in a pan. Pour in the reserved stock to cover about 1cm above the rice level. Add the salt and one-third of the onions and stir them together. Bring the rice to the boil for about 3 minutes to reduce the water down to the rice surface.

• Turn the heat down to low, cover the pan and cook for 15 minutes.

• Fold the lentils into the rice and simmer for another 5 minutes.

• Turn the *mdardara* onto a flat serving plate and spread the remaining onions over the top.

Butter Beans with Tomatoes
Fasoulia Bzeit

This is a very quick, simple and enjoyable way of cooking butter beans. I often have it sitting in my fridge to be served as tasty and satisfying snacks. Serve it with rice if served as a main dish. Also this dish is a perfect vegetable dish with any grilled meat.

SERVES 4

4 tbsp olive oil
1 large onion, chopped
4 garlic cloves, coarsely
   chopped
500g cooked butter beans
4 tomatoes, diced
30g fresh coriander, chopped
Salt and freshly ground black
   pepper

Preparation time: 15 minutes
Cooking time: 40 minutes

• Heat 3 tbsp of the oil and fry the onion and garlic until they are slightly brown.

• Add the beans and tomatoes, cover the pan and simmer on a low heat for 20 minutes.

• Add the coriander, season with salt and pepper and simmer for a further 5 minutes.

• After turning off the heat, stir in the remaining 1 tbsp olive oil.

Cook's tip
• Remember, no salt if cooking dried beans until they are well cooked.

Green Lentils with Caramelised Onions
Mjadara

This is just about the most peasant dish, you could imagine, it is so economical and popular. My students always loved this dish and used to say if they saw the recipe with so few simple and basic ingredients, they would never have tried it, but having to do it in class they surprised themselves and thoroughly enjoyed it. It is a simple recipe but must be followed closely to get the right texture and taste. Mjadara is preferred cold for better flavour and served with Cabbage Salad (page 74), mixed salad with Lebanese Salad Dressing (page 233), or/and Yoghurt and Cucumber Salad (page 68).

SERVES 4

250g green lentils
1.5 litres boiling water
50g long-grain rice
2 onions, chopped
100ml olive oil plus 1 tbsp
1 tsp salt

Preparation time: 10 minutes
Cooking time: 1¼–1½ hours

• Put the lentils in a pan with 1 litre boiling water, return to the boil, cover, then simmer on a low heat for 1 hour.

• Add the rice and continue to simmer until the lentils are soft and the rice looks almost dissolved. You may need to add more boiling water, but do so just a little at a time until everything is well cooked and looks creamy.

• Meanwhile, heat the olive oil and fry the onions until browned. Reserve a few for the garnish.

• Add the remaining onions to the lentils, stir in the salt and simmer for a few more minutes.

• After turning off the heat, stir in the 1 tbsp olive oil. Pour into a serving dish and allow to set before serving garnished with the reserved onions.

Dried Broad Beans with Lemony Dressing
Foul Mdammas

This dish is usually a traditional weekend breakfast. There are plenty of specialist shops you step into just to enjoy a bowl of *foul mdammas*. It is a tasty, healthy and extremely low-cost dish. You may find fava beans in some supermarkets and speciality shops. They are definitely worth finding and enjoying. Most of my recipes are for 4, but this one is for 2.

SERVES 2

220g dried broad beans
2 garlic cloves, crushed
1/2 tsp salt
2 tbsp lemon juice
1 tomato, chopped
2 tbsp chopped fresh parsley
2 tbsp olive oil

Serving suggestion
Pitta Bread (page 230)
Vegetables such as onions,
  radishes and fresh mint
Pickles

Preparation time: 15 minutes
Cooking time: 5 minutes

• Soak the beans in water overnight, then boil (without salt) for 1 hour until tender. Or use tinned beans, which are perfectly fine for a quick, simple meal.

• Put the cooked beans in a bowl and squash slightly with a spoon.

• Blend the crushed garlic, salt and lemon juice and mix with the beans.

• Turn onto a serving bowl and top with chopped tomatoes and parsley, then drizzle the olive oil over the top.

Warm Chickpeas with Lemon Dressing
Balila

Balila can be prepared in a matter of minutes. It is usually served with other dishes but it is filling enough to have on its own as a meal or a healthy snack, in which case this quantity would serve two people.

SERVES 2

300g well-cooked chickpeas
1 garlic clove, crushed
2 tbsp lemon juice
½ tsp salt
2 tbsp olive oil
1 tsp ground cumin

Preparation time: 15 minutes
Cooking time: 5 minutes

- Cover the chickpeas with boiling water, boil to heat through, then drain.

- Meanwhile, mix the crushed garlic with the lemon juice and salt. Stir into the chickpeas.

- Turn onto a deep dish, drizzle the olive oil over the top and sprinkle with the cumin.

Bulgur Wheat with Tomatoes
Burghul ma Banadoura

I grew up eating this peasant dish at least twice a week. You can eat this as it is, with salad, or sometimes it is served with other food as a rice substitute. We always enjoy it by itself. When we have *burghul* in the house we can always produce a meal even when there is nothing much else around.

SERVES 4

60ml olive oil
220g onions, chopped
450g ripe tomatoes, diced
1 tsp salt
120g coarse burghul (bulgur wheat)

Serving suggestion
Cabbage Salad (page 74) or Tomato and Red Onion Salad (page 78)

Preparation time: 10 minutes
Cooking time: 30 minutes

• Heat the oil and fry the onions until slightly brown.

• Add the tomatoes and salt and stir together. Turn the heat to low, cover the pan and simmer gently for 5 minutes so the tomatoes and onions cook in their own juices.

• Rinse the burghul, drain and add to the tomatoes. As soon as it boils, cover the pan, turn the heat down to low and simmer for 15 minutes until all the moisture has evaporated.

• Remove from the heat and serve hot.

Chickpeas with Garlic Yoghurt

Fatteh Hummus

Fatteh is usually served for breakfast and mostly in special breakfast cafès. It is light with delicious, refreshing flavours that you will enjoy eating at lunch or dinner too.

SERVES 4

150g Lebanese bread or pitta
2 tbsp oil
15g pine nuts
250g cooked chickpeas
1 garlic clove, crushed
400g plain yoghurt
1/2 tsp salt
Pinch of ground cumin

Preparation time: 30 minutes

• Split and cut the bread into small pieces, place on a baking tray and drizzle with a little of the oil, then toast in the oven to brown.

• Heat little more oil and fry the pine nuts to brown lightly.

• Place the toasted bread in the base of a glass bowl.

• Heat the chickpeas and spoon them on top of the toasted bread.

• Mix the crushed garlic with the yoghurt and salt, then pour over the top.

• Spread the pine nuts on top of the yoghurt and sprinkle with a pinch of ground cumin. Serve straight away.

Lentils with Pasta and Coriander

Mekassasa

This very delicious old-fashioned recipe has made a real come-back. Many Lebanese people would say they'd never heard of it unless they grew up in the mountains. It is a recipe where you can turn a few lentils and a bit of pasta into a very tasty meal.

SERVES 4

250g green or brown lentils
1.5 litres boiling water
120g plain flour, plus extra
  for rolling out
Pinch of salt
50ml water
50ml olive oil
250g onions, chopped
1 tsp salt
4 garlic cloves, crushed
40g coriander leaves

Serving suggestion
Mixed salad

Preparation time: 30–40
  minutes
Cooking time: 1¼ hours

* Put the lentils in a saucepan, pour in the boiling water, cover the pan and cook on a low heat for about 1 hour, depending on the variety, until they are well cooked.

* Mix the flour with a pinch of salt and add a little water at a time to make a soft dough, cover it and leave it to rest for 20 minutes.

* Heat two-thirds of the oil and fry the onions until golden brown.

* Add to the lentils with 1 tsp of salt and continue cooking.

* On a floured board, roll the pasta very thinly, cut into strips about 5cm long and gently drop them separately into the lentils so they don't stick together. Cook for a further 10 minutes.

* Heat the remaining oil, stir in the crushed garlic and chopped coriander leaves and cook for 2 minutes.

* Add to the lentils and cook for another 5 minutes.

* Turn into a serving dish and serve hot or cold.

Spicy Bean Patties
Falafel

Many people are familiar with falafel wraps as they have become very popular in the West. In Lebanon, as well as throughout the Middle East, falafel is the traditional number one street food, loved by everyone. People very rarely make falafel at home as it seems too complicated; but once you've made it you realise how simple it is. Ramzi, my brother who is a big fan of falafel, always makes his own falafel at home. In truth, I had never made it before (although I've eaten it throughout my life) but with Ramzi on the other end of the phone giving me instructions, I managed to get the recipe right and it tastes just the way it should. If you can't get dried broad beans, just use chickpeas.

SERVES 4

150g dried chickpeas
150g dried broad beans
1 onion, finely chopped
1 bulb garlic, separated and
   finely chopped
30g fresh coriander, chopped
20g fresh parsley, chopped
50g ground coriander
1 tsp freshly ground black
   pepper
60g plain flour
2 tsp baking powder
1 tsp salt
Oil, for frying

To serve
Chopped parsley, tomatoes
   and pickles
Pitta Bread (page 230) for
   making wraps
Simple Tahini Sauce (page
   232)

Preparation time: 50 minutes
Cooking time: 30 minutes

• Soak the chickpeas and beans overnight in cold water.

• Drain and finely chop in a blender so it looks like fine breadcrumbs.

• Mix all ingredients together very well and leave the mixture for a couple of hours. Fry the falafel only when you are ready to serve.

• Roll the falafel into small balls and squash a little between the palms of your hands.

• Heat the oil in a deep pan or a wok and fry 1 falafel, then remove it when it turns brown.

• Now turn the heat down to medium and slowly cook the rest so they are thoroughly cooked and crunchy on the outside. This will take about 30 minutes.

• Cook just what's required and it's perfectly okay to freeze the rest of the mixture.

• Serve with chopped parsley, tomatoes and pickles, if available, and serve hot with flatbread and tahini sauce to assemble your own wrap.

CHAPTER 6

Sweets

Hilwayat

Lebanese sweets are extremely sweet and therefore they are never part of a meal. Seasonal fruits are always placed on the table after a meal, but you never expect a dessert. Sweets are usually offered with coffee or as snacks.

Various types of sweets are offered on special religious occasions. There is even a specific dessert which is offered to visitors when they come to congratulate the family after a baby is born.

In Lebanon there are a number of patisseries in almost every street and they always seem busy. People stop for sweet snacks and it is also customary to take sweets with you when visiting. Most sweet pastries are bought commercially as they are usually made to a high standard, but in fact they are quite easy to make.

Nuts are always used – especially pine nuts, almonds, walnuts and pistachios – either for pastry filling or for decorating sweets. Filled pastries are always dipped or served in sugar syrup. Rose water (*maward*) and orange flower water (*mazaher*) are added to syrup, which give a fragrant and very special flavour.

Syrupy Filo and Nut Pastries

Baklawa

Patisseries sell such a wide variety of pastries, particularly *baklawa*, which come in all shapes and sizes. Patisseries vary in quality, but because there are so many patisseries you get to know the ones that make good *baklawa*. Because you can buy high-quality baklawa, people never make it at home, and that includes me, but in the UK I make *baklawa* at home because it's so easy and all my family prefer it to the commercial ones.

SERVES 4

300g walnuts
3 tbsp granulated sugar
1 tbsp orange flower water
1 tbsp rose water
400g melted butter
270g packet of filo pastry
200ml Aromatic Sugar Syrup
  (page 240)
1 tbsp ground pistachio nuts

Preparation time: 35 minutes
Cooking time: 45 minutes

- Preheat the oven to 180°C/Gas 4.

- Chop the walnuts in a food processor so they look like coarse breadcrumbs. Mix with the sugar, orange flower water and rose water.

- Melt the butter and use a little to grease the bottom and sides of a baking tin about 24x34x5cm. Set 50g of the butter to one side.

- Place the first sheet of filo pastry in the tin and brush with melted butter. Continue to use one-third of the pastry sheets in the same way, brushing with melted butter between the sheets.

- Evenly spread the filling over the pastry.

- Place the remaining pastry sheets on top of the nut mixture, brushing each sheet with melted butter until you have used all the filo sheets.

- With a sharp knife, cut the *baklawa* into squares or diamond shapes all the way through to the base of the tin.

- Finally drizzle remaining 50g of butter over the top.

- Bake in the oven for 45 minutes until the surface is golden brown.

- Remove from the oven, drizzle with the cooled sugar syrup and decorate each piece with crushed pistachio.

- Allow to cool, then arrange the individual pieces on a serving dish.

Cook's tip
- If the *baklawa* is not all served on the same day, cover it well and keep it in the fridge.

Walnut-filled Pancakes

Katayef

Katayef pancakes are very special during the month of Ramadan. They are available throughout the whole month in every patisserie. In Lebanon you can even just buy the pancakes for convenience and fill them at home so they are ready when required. They are usually filled with crushed walnuts, or sometimes with white unsalted cheese.

SERVES AT LEAST 6

For the pancakes
150g plain flour
1 tsp instant dried yeast
1 tsp sugar
300ml warm water
3 tbsp oil, for frying

For the filling
120g walnuts
40g granulated sugar
1 tbsp rose water
1 tbsp orange flower water
Aromatic Sugar Syrup (page 240)

Preparation time: 1 hour
Cooking time: 15–20 minutes

• Mix the flour, yeast, sugar and water and whisk until the batter-like mixture becomes creamy and lump free. Cover and leave it aside to ferment and form bubbles, approximately 1 hour.

• Meanwhile, prepare the filling by coarsely chopping the nuts in food processor to look like breadcrumbs.

• Add the sugar, rose water and orange flower water and mix well.

• To make the pancakes, heat a pan with a thick base, or a griddle if you have one. Drop 1 tbsp of the batter on the preheated surface. The pancakes are cooked when they bubble and dry on the surface, and the bottom of the pancakes should be very slightly brown. Cook only one side.

• Remove from the heat and place on waxed paper or baking parchment to cool. Continue to cook the pancakes until you have used the batter.

• Fill each pancake with 2 heaped tsp of the filling, fold and stick the edges firmly to keep the filling in.

• In a frying pan, heat a little oil and shallow-fry the pancakes to brown on each side until they are slightly crispy.

• When you remove each pancake from the pan, drop it in the syrup for a couple of minutes.

• Remove from the syrup and place the pancakes on a serving plate. Serve hot or warm.

Pancakes with Curd

Katayef be Kashta

This is another option for using *katayef* pancakes, which some people prefer. In this recipe you don't cook the pancakes again.

SERVES 4

12 *katayef* pancakes (page 202)
200g Milk Curd (page 238)
20g pistachio nuts, finely crushed
1 tbsp orange petal jam (optional)
150ml Aromatic Sugar Syrup (page 240)

Preparation time: 10 minutes

- Fill each of the pancakes with 2 tsp milk curd.

- Close half of the pancake by sticking the edges together to create a cone shape.

- Dip the open end in pistachios and decorate with orange petals, if liked.

- Serve with syrup.

Middle Eastern Caramelised Bread Pudding
Aysh al Saraya

Most countries have their own version of bread pudding in one way or another. You can never buy this sweet in any patisserie, but can only have it made at home. It is very sweet, very sticky and extremely simple and delicious.

SERVES 4

300g sliced white bread, about 7 thick slices
450g granulated sugar
150ml hot water
1 tsp lemon juice
1 tbsp orange flower water
1 tbsp rose water
170g Milk Curd (page 238) of 1 litre whole milk
150g whipped cream
Crushed pistachio nuts

Preparation time: 1 hour plus chilling

• After cutting off all the crusts, toast the bread very lightly just to dry it but not brown it. Cut into small piece and spread on a flat serving dish.

• Put the sugar in a pan and allow it to melt on a low heat while stirring all the time to caramelise.

• When the sugar begins to turn brown, immediately remove the pan from the heat and very carefully add the water, which will make the sugar bubble vigorously.

• Return the pan to the heat, add the lemon juice and allow the syrup to boil for 10 minutes. Test a few drops on a cold plate. If it thickens when cold, then it's ready.

• Add the rose water and orange flower water to the syrup and pour over the bread. Leave to cool, then keep in the fridge for 6 hours before serving.

• Mix the curd with the cream and spread it over the bread, then sprinkle with the crushed pistachio.

Cook's tip
• This dessert is so simple, but it can be ruined by overcooking the sugar, which can quickly burn and result in a burnt sugar taste. Therefore make sure that you keep an eye on it and remove it from the heat as soon as it begins to brown.

Filled Cakes with Dates or Nuts
Maamool

Maamool are made with semolina dough filled either with walnuts, pistachio nuts or dates. They are usually offered with coffee during any festivity, especially at Easter. They are seriously delicious and keep for weeks in any airtight container.

SERVES 8–10

For the dough
350g coarse semolina
300g fine semolina or plain flour
1 tsp instant dried yeast
400g unsalted butter, melted
2 tbsp rose water
2 tbsp orange flower water
4 tbsp water

For the fillings
150g walnuts or pistachio nuts, chopped
40g granulated sugar
1 tbsp orange flower water (mazaher)
1 tbsp rose water
250g moist variety of stoned dates, minced
50ml warm water
Icing sugar, for dusting

Preparation time: 1½ hours
Cooking time: 40 minutes

• In a bowl, mix the semolina, flour and yeast. Add the melted butter, rose water, orange flower water and water. Mix well to form a dough. Cover and leave the dough for at least 10 hours.

• Preheat the oven to 190°C/Gas 5 and line a baking sheet with baking parchment.

• Mix all the filling ingredients together so the mixtures hold together like a paste.

• Loosen the dough and knead to soften, then break into pieces the size of golf balls. Flatten the dough between the palm of your hands and place 1 tsp of the filling and seal the dough round it. Place on the baking tray, keeping space between the cakes. Pattern the surface with a special *maamool* mould or just use a fork.

• Bake in the oven for 40 minutes.

• After removing from the oven, dust thickly with icing sugar and allow to cool completely before removing from the tray. This is to avoid crumbling.

Cook's tip
• People always add butter to the dates because dates can get dry after baking, so because of the quantity of butter in the pastry, I decided to add warm water to the dates to replace the butter. This worked well, reduced the fat and the dates were very moist after baking. Do not dust the date version as they are naturally sweet enough – great for people who don't eat sugar.

Date and Nut Squares

Maamool Madd

These date or nut slices have the same ingredients as *maamool*, but surprisingly they taste completely different. *Maamool Madd* is simple and great to offer guests with coffee or tea and it keeps for at least a week. These are also made with a walnut or pistachio filling like *maamool*, in which case simply follow the same method.

SERVES AT LEAST 6

300g fine semolina
1 tsp instant dried yeast
160g unsalted butter, melted
$\frac{1}{2}$ tbsp rose water
$\frac{1}{2}$ tbsp orange flower water
450g stoned dates
50ml hot water

Preparation time: 30 minutes
Cooking time: 45 minutes

- Mix the semolina with yeast. Add the melted butter, rose water and orange flower water to the semolina and mix well with your hands so all the semolina looks wet.

- Cover this dough and leave for a day or two so it becomes doughy and well soaked.

- Preheat the oven to 180°C/Gas 4 and grease and line a 25x25cm baking tin.

- Mince the dates either with a knife or a food processor, adding the hot water to mix well and soften.

- Spread half the semolina mix in the baking tin and press down firmly. Cover with the dates, then firmly spread the remaining semolina over the top.

- Bake in the oven for 45 minutes until the surface is golden brown.

- Allow to cool and set completely before slicing and removing from the tin.

Sweet Almond Fingers
Asabe Louz

This is another variety of *baklawa*, except this version is made with almonds rolled in filo pastry. Different shapes seem to have a different taste.

SERVES AT LEAST 6

250g almonds, finely chopped
3 tbsp sugar
1 tbsp orange flower water
1 tbsp rose water
100g butter, melted
270g packet of filo pastry
4 tbsp Aromatic Sugar Syrup (page 240)
15g chopped pistachio

Preparation time: 30 minutes
Cooking time: 45 minutes

• Preheat the oven to 180°C/Gas 4.

• Prepare the filling by mixing the almonds with the sugar, orange flower water and rose water.

• Brush a flat baking tray with melted butter.

• Unfold the filo and cut the sheets in half. Using 3 sheets of filo for each roll, take one sheet at a time, brush with butter, then place the next one on top and brush again. Spread with 3 tsp of the almond filling and roll as in the photographs. Place on the baking tray and cut the rolls 5cm long without separating them. Brush the surface with butter.

• Bake in the oven for 45 minutes.

• Remove from the oven, drizzle with the cooked sugar syrup and sprinkle the pistachio nuts over the top.

Sweet Spiced Rice Dessert
Meghli

This is the most traditional dessert in Lebanon. It is only offered to well wishers who visit when a baby is born. The custom is to offer *meghli* for six weeks after the birth, so every few days a new batch will be prepared. It is always served with mixed nuts on top. Some people express their wealth and generosity by the generous amount and quality of the nuts. It's a great dish for cinnamon lovers. I wrote this recipe in a busy *meghli* time to celebrate the birth of my granddaughter Florence (see photo below).

SERVES 4

Handful of walnuts,
  almonds, pistachio nuts
  and pine nuts
150g ground rice
150g sugar
15g ground cinnamon
3g ground aniseed
3g ground caraway seeds
1/2 tsp ground ginger
1 litre cold water
1 tbsp desiccated coconut
  (optional)

Preparation time: 10 minutes
Cooking time: 1 1/2 hours

• You may use some or all of the different nuts. Soak them in cold water for 1–2 hours. They will swell and look fresh, and the flavour is improved.

• Mix the rice and sugar with all the spices and place in a pan. Blend in the water and stir until there are no lumps, then keep stirring over a medium heat until it starts boiling.

• Turn the heat down to low and keep stirring frequently for about 1 hour. (Be careful as it will bubble.) After 1 hour the rice should be cooked and the mixture rich, brown and thick.

• Divide between individual bowls and allow to cool.

• Sprinkle with the coconut, if you like.

• Drain the nuts and sprinkle over the rice. Keep in the fridge until required.

The author with granddaughter Florence for whom she made Meghli.

Semolina and Yoghurt Cake

Nammoura

Nammoura is one of the oldest recipes but the Lebanese people have never stopped buying or making it. As children with very little pocket money, we could only afford to buy *nammoura* from the street seller, so I've always loved this very sweet and sticky aromatic cake and still do.

SERVES 6–10

15–20 almonds depending
  on the size of pieces
150g unsalted butter
160g granulated sugar
350g fine semolina
2 tsp baking powder
200g plain yoghurt
1 tbsp tahini
1 tbsp melted butter
300ml Aromatic Sugar Syrup
  (page 240)

Preparation time: 15 minutes
  plus soaking
Cooking time: 45 minutes

- Soak the almonds in boiling water for 1 hour, then remove from water and peel off the skins.

- Preheat the oven to 180°C/Gas 4.

- Cream the butter with the sugar.

- Add the semolina and baking powder to the mixture and mix well. Add the yoghurt and blend well with the semolina mix.

- Grease an approximately 22x32 cm baking tin with the tahini and spread the semolina mixture evenly in the tin with the back of a spoon. Score the top of the mixture into squares or diamonds with a knife and place an almond on each piece.

- Bake in the oven for 45 minutes.

- Remove from the oven and brush the surface with melted butter, then return to the oven for 2 minutes.

- While still in the baking tin, cut into pieces along the scored lines and pour the cold sugar syrup all over the cake and allow to cool before you transfer it onto a serving plate.

Syrupy Aniseed and Walnut Pastries
Mghattas

When I stayed at home to look after my old grandmother, we often made *mghattas* because it was our favourite sweet dish. This rural recipe and old-fashioned recipe was always made for the family and guests and never bought ready made. Apart from being popular, people always had these ingredients available in the cupboard, enough to produce this delicious pastry.

SERVES 4–6

For the pastry
300g plain flour, plus extra
  for rolling out
1 tsp baking powder
3 tsp aniseed
100g olive oil
100ml cold water

For the filling
200g walnuts
60g sugar
1 tbsp orange flower water

Oil, for deep-frying
500ml Aromatic Sugar Syrup
  (page 240)

Preparation time: 30–50
  minutes, plus chilling
Cooking time: 20 minutes

• Mix the flour, baking powder and aniseed, then add the oil and mix to a crumble. Add a little cold water at a time until you have a soft pastry, cover and leave it in the fridge for 30 minutes.

• Crush the walnuts in a food processor or just simply place them in a tea towel and crush them with a rolling pin, then mix with the sugar and orange flower water.

• Roll the pastry to about 3mm thick and cut into 12cm diameter circles with a glass or pastry cutter.

• Place 1 heaped tsp of filling on one side of each circle and fold. Press the edges firmly, then pinch and twist from one corner to the other.

• Heat the oil in a deep pan and fry the pastries for about 20 minutes to brown.

• When removed from the oil, drop each one into the syrup to soak for few minutes before placing on a serving dish.

Rice and Cheese Dessert

Halawet Rouz

The first time I saw this desert was at a patisserie, and it looked so appetising I had a portion and really loved it. I was curious to have the recipe, which I didn't think they would give me. I asked to see the chef to complement him on his lovely recipe, we had a chat and he was happy to give details of the ingredients. Being a Lebanese chef, he loved to share his knowledge of good food. Sometimes this dessert is served with syrup on the side for those with a very sweet tooth. It is also sometimes decorated with orange petal jam, if available.

SERVES 4

80g pudding rice
600ml whole milk
60g icing sugar
1 tbsp rose water
1 tbsp orange flower water
220g ball of mozzarella
   cheese, grated

To decorate
4 tbsp Milk Curd (page 238)
1 tbsp ground pistachio nuts

Preparation time: 10 minutes
Cooking time: 1¼ hours

- Mix the rice and milk in a pan and gently cook on low heat for about 1 hour until the rice is mushy and well cooked.

- Purèe the rice in a blender. Return to the heat and add the icing sugar, stirring continuously. Add the rose water, orange flower water and cheese, stirring for another 5 minutes.

- Turn into a serving dish or small individual dishes and leave to cool.

- Spoon the curd over the top, decorate with sprinkled pistachio nuts and serve cold.

Cheese and Semolina Rolls
Halawet El Jebin

This is a speciality of the north of Lebanon (around Tripoli) and is rarely sold at patisseries anywhere else in the country. It is very quick and simple and a good dessert or just to offer with coffee. Orange flower jam can be found in Lebanese stores or online.

SERVES AT LEAST 6

2 x 220g balls of mozzarella
3 tbsp rose water
2 tbsp orange flower water
4 tbsp Aromatic Sugar Syrup, plus extra for serving (page 240)
50g semolina
1 tbsp ground pistachio nuts
Orange flower jam (optional)
Milk Curd (page 238)

Preparation time: 1 hour

• Cut the cheese into small pieces, place in a pan on a low heat and allow it to melt.

• Add the rose water, orange flower water, 2 tbsp of the syrup and the semolina, stirring all the time for 5 minutes. In that time the semolina is cooked and has absorbed any moisture. It should look like a ball of dough.

• Spread a little syrup on the worktop and quickly roll out the dough while it is still warm as thinly as you can, almost paper thin. Cut it into 6–7cm squares, fill with 1 tsp of the curd and roll up.

• After arranging on a serving plate, sprinkle with ground pistachio and decorate with a little orange flower jam, if liked. Serve with syrup.

Dried Fruit Salad

Khashaf

This wintery, old-fashioned fruit salad is always popular throughout the Middle East. It is prepared well in advance to allow the fruit to soak up all the delicate flavours.

SERVES 4

100g dried apricots
200g dried figs
150g prunes
100g seedless raisins
100g sultanas
60g halved almonds
30g pine nuts
1 tbsp rose water
$\frac{1}{2}$ tbsp orange flower water
3cm cinnamon stick

To decorate
A few chopped pistachio
   nuts

Preparation time: 30 minutes
   plus soaking

• Chop half the apricots and soak in warm water overnight.

• Purèe in a blender, adding a little more water if it's too thick. It should look like a thick fruit juice.

• Chop the figs, prunes and remaining apricots into halves. Add to the remaining ingredients and mix with the purèed apricots. Cover and leave to soak for a day or so.

• Serve in individual small dishes and sprinkle chopped pistachio over the top just before serving.

CHAPTER 7

Basic Recipes
Aklaat Asasiyeh

This section of the book provides you with a few basic recipes that are often used in Lebanese cuisine, so you'll find references to this section throughout the book.

The ingredients for this section are very basic and very commonly used, such as tahini, vermicelli and, of course, olive oil, which is always essential in Lebanese cooking. These ingredients are always found in the Lebanese kitchen as they are used all the time. Since they have a long shelf life, don't hesitate to buy a one litre jar of tahini when you see it in specialised shops – it will be much better value and once you have become a fan of Lebanese cooking, you will go through a lot of tahini.

Yoghurt (*laban*) is always made in large quantities because it is used regularly. No Lebanese fridge is ever without a big pot of yoghurt. It is always better to use mature yoghurt for cooking, and it will keep in the fridge for up to two weeks.

Bread is very important. The Lebanese can't survive without their bread. If you get round to making Lebanese bread, which you can keep in your freezer, you'll never buy commercially made pitta bread again.

Syrup is quick and simple to make but it is important to have good-quality *mazaher* (orange flower water) and *maward* (rose water) always kept in your cupboard (not the concentrates). They are bought in 500ml bottles and will keep for at least two years.

Lebanese Rice with Vermicelli
Rouz be Shayreyeh

Sometimes we serve plain rice, but mostly we cook rice with vermicelli, sometimes called angel hair pasta, and it's tasty even to eat on its own. Use ordinary long-grain rice rather than basmati; I never cook basmati rice with vermicelli because Basmati rice has a unique flavour and scent and vermicelli would overpower the taste. People can often judge your cooking by the quality of your rice, so it's important to get it right! The important thing is never to serve sticky rice.

SERVES 4

400g long-grain rice
20g butter or oil
60g vermicelli (angel hair),
  lightly crushed
1/2 tsp salt

Cooking time: 20 minutes

• Rinse the rice a few times, then leave to soak in warm water for 30 minutes to 1 hour if you have enough time. This is a key step to prevent sticking.

• Heat the butter or oil in a large pan and stir-fry the noodles for 2–3 minutes until they just turn golden brown.

• Drain the rice and stir it into the noodles.

• Add the salt and pour in enough water to come 1cm above the rice level. (If you haven't soaked the rice, then top it by 2cm.) Bring to the boil, then simmer for about 3 minutes until most of the water has evaporated from the surface.

• Now cover the rice, turn the heat down to very low and leave to simmer for about 15 minutes, giving the rice a quick stir once or twice, until all the excess moisture has evaporated.

• If the rice is still slightly undercooked, just add very little water and cook for a few more minutes.

Pitta Bread
Khibez

This bread is actually very easy to make. We always serve bread with Lebanese food – it's essential for dipping and for scooping certain foods, and is the main carbohydrate in the Lebanese diet. While I was waiting at the local bakery, Fourn El Barakeh in Baakline, I photographed the bread rising in the oven.

SERVES 4

500g strong plain or
   wholemeal flour, plus extra
   for rolling out
1 sachet instant dried yeast
1 tsp salt
About 250ml warm water

Preparation time: 40 minutes
Cooking time: 30 minutes

• Mix the flour with the yeast and salt, then gradually add enough water to create a smooth, non-sticky dough. Knead the dough until it becomes smooth without any flour pockets.

• Place the dough in an oiled bowl – bearing in mind that it will double its size when risen – cover with a wet damp towel and keep in a warm place or at just room temperature for 2 hours until doubled in size.

• Preheat the oven to maximum and place a thick, flat baking sheet or an oven tray in the oven.

• Knead the dough again, divide into pieces about the size of a tennis ball or smaller and roll into balls.

• Roll out each one on a lightly floured surface to a flat circle 1–2cm thick. Sprinkle with flour and allow to rest for few minutes.

• Now begin baking. Placing 1 or 2 loaves on the heated surface, allowing a little space between them, and put them in the hot oven.

• After about 10 minutes, the heat splits and puffs up the bread and turns it slightly golden. Remove the bread from the oven and cover the loaves with a cloth to avoid drying. Continue with the remaining bread.

Cook's tip
• I make a large batch to freeze. After baking, just stack them in a pile and push the air out so it doesn't take too much space in your freezer.

Simple Tahini Sauce

Tarator

Tahini – or sesame cream – is one of our main ingredients. A Lebanese kitchen is never without tahini. It is mostly used as a sauce, or combined with other ingredients for dips. Sometimes it is also used in cooking as the main sauce. This basic sauce is always served with fish, falafel and fried or roasted cauliflower. You can vary this sauce by adding chopped parsley or sometimes chopped tomatoes and parsley. Some people use tahini sauce for salad dressing, what we call Farmer's Salad.

MAKES 250ML

3 tbsp lemon juice
100g light tahini
About 100ml cold water
1 garlic clove, crushed
½ tsp salt

Preparation time: 10 minutes

• Add the lemon juice to the tahini and mix by hand. You will notice that the mixture becomes thick and fluffy.

• Now start adding cold water a little at a time and continue the hand blending. Keep on adding and blending until the mixture becomes as thick as cream and there are no lumps in the sauce.

• Add the crushed garlic and salt.

Cook's tips
• It is important to begin the mix with tahini and lemon juice and never with water. This is because tahini is a heavy ingredient, which reacts to the lemon and becomes fluffy. If you add water first, it stops the fluffiness and changes the consistency of the sauce. If you change the order it's made, it will totally change the taste.

• How thin you make it depends on how you use it: thin for salad dressing and thicker for sauce to serve with cauliflower or with fish.

Lebanese Salad Dressing

Salsa Salata Lebnaneyeh

Lebanese salad dressing is a very simple blend of garlic, lemon, salt and olive oil. Occasionally wine vinegar is used instead of lemon. It is very important to serve salad with some of the dishes and especially when recommended with dryer dishes. This salad dressing is used because the flavours are complementary to the flavours in Lebanese food.

SERVES 4

2 tbsp lemon juice
1 tbsp olive oil
1 garlic clove, crushed
¼ tsp salt

Preparation time: 5 minutes

- Mix all ingredients together thoroughly.
- Pour over your chosen salad and toss together well.

Cook's tip
- Some salads will need more dressing than others. If I am serving Cabbage Salad (page 74), for example, then I'll use the above quantity. If I am serving a moister salad such as Tomato and Red Onion Salad (page 78), then less dressing is required. It's up to you to taste and judge for yourself.

Pickled Baby Aubergines with Garlic and Walnuts
Makdoos

This unique pickle is very strong in flavour, very popular and present in most Lebanese houses. It is served as a starter or as a side dish, or it can be sandwiched in any bread. *Makdoos* is quite simple to make and, like any other pickles, it keeps for a year, although it is better in a fridge, otherwise the aubergines may go a little soft.

MAKES ABOUT 12

500g small baby aubergines
70g walnuts, finely chopped
  like breadcrumbs
6 garlic cloves, chopped
2 chillies, chopped (optional)
1 tsp salt
Olive oil

Preparation time: 1 hour
  plus drying

• Bring a pan of water to the boil, add the aubergines, return to the boil and blanch for 5 minutes. They should soften slightly, but not be too soft.

• Remove them from the water and place them separately on absorbent kitchen paper or a tea towel.

• Slit the aubergines vertically down the middle and allow them to dry for 5–6 hours.

• Prepare the filling by mixing the nuts with the garlic, chillies and salt.

• Fill each aubergine with 1 tsp of the filling and press the sides together before stacking them in a jar. Make sure they are stacked with the cut-side up so the filling doesn't fall out.

• Pour in enough olive oil to cover all the aubergines.

• Place the lid on tightly and allow to stand for at least 3 weeks before they are ready to eat. Make sure the aubergines are under the surface of the oil as this ensures they keep in good condition.

Home-made Yoghurt
Tarweeb Laban

Making yoghurt is a simple and most rewarding experience. Every time I lift the lid after adding the culture and see it beginning to set, I still get the same satisfaction as the first time! Apart from being cheaper than buying it ready made, it's so much better for natural flavour. We use a large amount of yoghurt as a salad, for cooking, and also for turning into cream cheese (labneh).

MAKES ABOUT 2 LITRES

2 litres semi-skimmed or full-fat milk
1 small carton plain yoghurt

Preparation time: 15 minutes plus settling

• Bring the milk to the boil in a saucepan, stirring occasionally. Keep an eye on it and when it just starts to boil and begin to rise, remove the pan from the heat.

• Allow the milk to cool to blood temperature. The simplest, unsophisticated but most effective way to check is to dip your little finger in the milk and count to ten. If your finger just starts to register slightly warm, then the milk is ready for the next step. If you feel too much heat before you get to ten, then allow it to cool a little more.

• When the temperature is right (body temperature), add the yoghurt and keep stirring till all the little lumps have dissolved.

• Cover the saucepan with a tight-fitting lid, then with a small towel and keep somewhere warm (an airing cupboard or near a radiator). Leave it undisturbed for about 8 hours or overnight. It is very important to keep yoghurt undisturbed during culture.

• Once it has set, transfer to the fridge to cool before serving. It will keep in the fridge for up to 2 weeks.

Milk Curd

Kashta

Kashta is an important ingredient in several Lebanese sweet dishes. It sounds daunting to make your own curd, but in fact it is quick and easy and you can keep it in the fridge for a few days. It is much lighter than cream, but sometimes the curd is too crumbly and set, so it is usually mixed with soft whipped cream as two-thirds kashta and one-third whipped cream.

MAKES 500G

2 litres whole milk
Juice of 1 lemon

Serving suggestion
Serve with honey

Preparation time: 20 minutes
Cooking time: 5 minutes

- Bring the milk to the boil in a large saucepan over a medium to low heat. If boiled on high heat, the milk will catch and ruin the flavour.

- Keep an eye on the milk so it doesn't boil over, and when it just begins to boil and rise, add the lemon juice and stir gently.

- Continue to stir for 1–2 minutes and the milk will begin to separate.

- Now start scooping off the curd from the surface of the milk with a slotted spoon and placing it on a sieve.

- Allow to drain, then cool, then keep it in the fridge.

Aromatic Sugar Syrup
Kator

The majority of Lebanese sweets require sugar syrup. Some are cooked, then drizzled with syrup; others are served with syrup on the side. I scent my syrup with rose water (*maward*) and orange flower water (*mazaher*).

MAKES 400ML

400g sugar
200ml hot water
1 tsp lemon juice
1 tbsp rose water
1 tbsp orange flower water

Cooking time: 25 minutes

• Combine the sugar, hot water and lemon juice in a pan over a low heat until the sugar has dissolved. Raise the heat to medium and bring to the boil, then boil for 15–20 minutes until the syrup has thickened.

• Spoon a little of the syrup onto a cold plate to test if it thickens when cold. If it turns thicker and sticky, then it's ready, otherwise allow it to boil for few more minutes.

• When it is ready, remove from the heat and add the rose water and orange flower water.

• Allow to cool before use. Store in the fridge for up to a few weeks.

Cook's tip
• Don't use the rose water or orange flower water from the supermarket as they don't have the same flavour. Try to track down some extracts that are sold in larger bottles, usually 500ml, which you will find in Greek or Cypriot shops or online.